Already Whole

Also by the Author:

Finding Lina: A Mother's Journey from Autism to Hope

Beyond Autism: My Life with Lina

Already Whole

DISCOVERING
THE SACRED WITHIN

Helena Hjalmarsson, MA, LCSW, LP

Skyhorse Publishing

Skyhorse Publishing books may be purchased in bulk at special discounts for sales promotion, corporate gifts, fund-raising, or educational purposes. Special editions can also be created to specifications. For details, contact the Special Sales Department, Skyhorse Publishing, 307 West 36th Street, 11th Floor, New York, NY 10018 or info@skyhorsepublishing.com.

Skyhorse® and Skyhorse Publishing® are registered trademarks of Skyhorse Publishing, Inc.®, a Delaware corporation.
Visit our website at www.skyhorsepublishing.com

10 9 8 7 6 5 4 3 2 1

Library of Congress Cataloging-in-Publication Data is available on file.

Cover design by Brian Peterson
Cover photograph by Helena Hjalmarsson

Print ISBN: 978-1-5107-6916-8
Ebook ISBN: 978-1-5107-6930-4

Printed in the United States of America

To Lina, who never ceases to amaze me with her kindness and deeply intelligent, mysterious, and truly original style. Her indomitable commitment to alignment and to helping those who suffer in isolated places, helps me remember my own sacred nature.

To Elsa, channeler of all that is good on this planet and beyond. She defies gravity with her awe-inspiring joy, groundbreaking poetry, enlightened dance moves, and chaotic, no-nonsense, live cooking shows.

To Scott Huber, whose steady, patient, and loving support for our whole family all these years made a deep impression on all of us.

Contents

INTRODUCTION

Soft, quiet footsteps
Slow, Spacious breath
Releasing, Relinquishing
Extending, Expanding
Everything Alive

No withholding
No asserting or arguing
No convincing or cajoling
No wrong, no right
Just Simple, Irresistible Life

Like a whale in the Ocean
Erupting out of Vastness
Its giant body suddenly defying Gravity

A glittering cascade of water and mammal
The Whole and the Free in the world

This is the land of Sacred Colors
Where Eagles stroll and Elephants fly
Where Flowers rain from Heaven

And Coyotes swim in the Ocean
Water and Sky Inseparable

Life experience can vary so wildly from one individual to another. Few would argue against the idea that every human being's ultimate desire is to be happy and free and—like the whale, powerfully breaching out of the deep waters up toward the sky—we strive not to be condemned by the laws of gravity. And yet, most people consider forces outside themselves to determine the quality of their lives. It is my hope that this book will help you realize the freedom and exuberant joy of being alive. That you may have opportunities to clarify who you are and find ways to live in the grace of that awareness for more hours of your days and nights. The purpose of this book is not to repair, redeem, fix, invent, or find anything. It is about tuning in to something that is *already there*. It is the recognition that no alterations are necessary for a full, happy, satisfying life, characterized less by limitation, adapting, and overcoming, and more by expansiveness, wholeness, and love.

Rumi beautifully illustrates this revolutionary, yet simple awareness of oneness, love, and awe in his poem "Quietness." He describes the quiet awareness of who we really are, opening our eyes to the miracle of life. The moment we stop trying to chase it down, when we let go of our hectic attempts to get where we want to be, life shows itself to us. "Your old life was a frantic running from silence" he wrote, "The speechless full moon comes out now."

How do we find the speechless full moon in a world that keeps telling us it doesn't exist or, at best, if it does exist, it's not important or can't be found without paying a price that more or less matches the reward? And if we find it, how do we share what we found? Well, Gorgias, one of the Sophist philosophers in Athens some four hundred years before Christ, would say it's an aspiration waiting to fail. He would go so far as to say *nothing* exists and even if it did, it couldn't be known, and even if it could be known it couldn't be shared. If he is right, this book, and every other book, and every other thought, insight, statement, philosophy, religion, and any other approach to find truth and well-being would be quite futile.

Lina, my oldest daughter, now eighteen, has autism. Her expressive language has failed her since she was three and a half years old. Via the letter boards that we use these days to communicate, I asked her what she thought of Gorgias's claims. My sophisticated, philosophically inclined teenager, with a hint of a smile almost undetectable on her beautiful face, wrote that she thought it was "reasonable." But then she told me that she indeed does believe that there are universal truths that *can* be known, one of them being that "beauty comes from love."

Personally, I'm with Lina. Love can be known and all the beauty in all the world comes from it. But as far as most other matters, thoughts, statements, beliefs, experiences—all the stuff that we count as real and feel we should agree on, I think Gorgias *and* Lina are onto something. The ultimate truth isn't something we can grasp with our minds. We have gotten a lot of things backward. What we consider real—the corporeal world—just how real, and valuable, is it? And what about all the stuff we discount as hocus-pocus, new age and lofty, half-crazy, a little out there? What does dismissing all that do for us? Is it possible that we have made our lives so noisy and overwhelming, packed with sensory information, and driven by evidence and facts that we missed the most fundamental part? The part that we can only find by quieting down and learning how to be truly receptive, beyond our thoughts? Most of us have real difficulty even recognizing what is at stake in *not* finding this kind of receptivity. Many people live their entire lives oblivious to silence and true peace. That too, ultimately, is okay, I think, because they will find it when they die. But if we want to discover it here, while we are alive on this planet, so often distracted by our physical lives, aspirations, fears, desires—we have to slow down a little. We have to start walking on a different path than the one we are used to, supported not by data and analytical thought, but by stillness and intuition. We need to be open to our intuition and ready to let go of the things that keep us separated from that openness. To take steps in that direction requires that we let opinions, preconceived ideas, experiences, personal habits, and inclinations fade into the background and allow ourselves to quiet down. We need to be willing to leave behind notions of thoughts and behaviors, ideas and beliefs, that we have learned to consider real and important and even responsible.

In 1930, Einstein wrote a credo that he called "What I Believe." He was trying to explain what he meant by calling himself religious:

> *The most beautiful thing we can experience is the mysterious. It is the source of all true art and science. He to whom this emotion is a stranger, who can no longer pause to wonder and stand rapt in awe, is as good as dead: his eyes are closed. This insight into the mystery of life, coupled though it be with fear, has also given rise to religion. To know that what is impenetrable to us really exists, manifesting itself as the highest wisdom and the most radiant beauty which our dull faculties can comprehend only in their most primitive forms—this knowledge, this feeling, is at the center of true religiousness. In this sense, and in this sense only, I belong in the ranks of devoutly religious men.*

To Einstein, the most important function of art and science was to awaken the feeling of the "mystery of life's eternity" and keep it alive.

This kind of receptivity requires that we stop our incessant habit of demanding that life somehow proves itself to us before we allow ourselves to listen. This is difficult for most of us to do. And yet, every new invention, every new creation begins with someone trusting something that's not yet perceivable on the outside. So why not make our whole life that creative?

Rumi comes very close to describing the things that go beyond what we think we know in his famous poem "Thirsty Fish," where he writes, "Show me the way to the ocean! / Break these half measures, these small containers." Those things, which are beyond the concrete and tangible, would leave us liberated if we really understood them. But ultimately, language doesn't suffice to describe this, because the notion goes so far beyond language and thought that we simply cannot fully comprehend it with our minds. We keep trying anyway. We try with words, music, art, touch. And while I do think that everything is here to support us in our journey toward freedom, I believe that ultimately, it's not about trying. It's about *not* trying. It's about allowing all those things that we are conditioned to think of as real to come and go. They are just thoughts, words, emotion, sensation. They can fly around as they please, like leaves in the autumn wind. We are not obliged to create some kind of conspiracy theory about them or put them in context. Nothing is as serious as we have come to believe. We can make choices about what to focus on, what to think about and what to say and how to feel about things and about each other. We can teach ourselves how to live close to our true home, in harmony with our true self and the pure love that holds no grudges, regrets nothing, and condemns no one.

Rumi's theory of language is that it exists because we are separated from the source. In his view, all language, all expression, is born out of a kind of longing for home. This book is motivated by that longing. It's an invitation to experience the "speechless full moon" and learn about our own power, our own love and absolute ability to live happily and harmoniously most of the time. I believe that we can, at any point of our lives, regardless of what is going on around us, tap into who we truly are.

How do we do that? How can we be in our most natural, most true state, connected with everything around us? Who can guide us toward greater freedom? The most universal guiding principles are powerfully demonstrated in nature. It doesn't matter what part of nature we study, everything in it teaches us how to live our lives in more vital, vibrant, fluid ways. There is a balance in nature, between holding on and letting go. There is a circular movement of birth and death. There is rising and falling. There is complete, full-blown, colorful, magnificent glory and cold, naked, straightforward, bold simplicity. Particularly in the Western world, however, as we live more and more disconnected from nature, we seem to have trouble understanding and living in harmony with these principles, and often, these struggles leave us feeling miserable, depressed, trapped, and fearful.

We try to control things, ourselves, each other, our environments, rather than enjoying and allowing and flowing with the genius of the universe. I believe that we are beings of energy and that our lives, days, and moments are determined by where we are energetically. None of our experiences, or our reactions to those experiences, are permanent. All the stuff that we habitually identify as us—our thoughts, feelings, experiences, sensations, moods—change all the time. None of it is fixed. None is inevitable or unmalleable. Our innermost true self—the part of us that some call "pure awareness" or "grace" or "Source" or even our "God self," or "Daimon," as Socrates called it—is the only thing that doesn't change. When we understand what is real and unchangeable and what isn't, energy begins to flow more freely in our everyday lives.

I will describe ways that energy can be blocked when we hold on too tightly to what is not real. I will focus on some of those areas that hold immense struggle for a lot of people, and, much more importantly, huge opportunity for all. These areas are all connected and ultimately inseparable from each other, but for reasons of accessibility I have tried to break them up into chapters. The first chapter describes some of my own, very personal experiences of places where I found love, grace, and inspiration. Chapters 2 through 6 are focused on subjects from "living from the inside" to magic. Chapter 7 holds some thoughts about silence and stillness. Throughout, I have added stories and reflections about people and situations that I have come across in my life in general as well as in my work as a psychotherapist over the years, hoping that they will help illustrate the concepts discussed in the main chapters. These people, whether they were clients, friends, or family, have all been meaningful to me in my own search for freedom and I hope they will help bring to life some of the ideas in this book. The eighth chapter, entitled Inspired and Awake, describes two individuals and one dog—all of whom I have had the opportunity to observe and get to know very closely. All three of them strike me as inspirational and awake beings on this planet. Without much noticeable effort, they all seem to have mastered various aspects of the concepts discussed in this book.

I believe that everyone alive is invited by the divine to live freely and harmoniously in every area of their lives. I don't think it matters if you call it the divine or if you choose not to call it anything. I also don't think it's more accessible to those who've had a difficult life or an easy one or something in between. We don't earn freedom through suffering or from enormous effort of will or intellect. It's not about being deserving or undeserving. We either realize who we are and how we can live free, connected, joyful and expansive lives or we don't. We can realize it some of the time and live a little bit connected and a little bit trapped, or we can learn to realize it most of the time and spend most of our lives fully awake. It's not up to our childhoods or our diagnoses or our current bosses or our wives or ex-husbands or the weather or our bank accounts. It has nothing to do with all that. It's naked, open, and straightforward. It just is.

1

Mother Earth and My North Stars

Don't remind the world that it's sick and troubled
Remind it that it's beautiful and free.
—Mooji (Jamaican spiritual teacher of non-dualism)

F OR AS LONG as I can remember, I have had a strong desire to find joy and freedom, regardless of circumstances. I saw early on in my childhood how suffering and sickness were experienced on deep levels by many of the people central in my life. And that the paths that lead to the search for truth and liberation are different from one person to another. Ultimately, I suspect that we all want the same thing. We want to live in harmony with who we truly are. For me, my desire was propelled by a combination of things. Most profoundly, it was the direct experiences of love that revealed itself to me at some of my darkest moments. It does seem that it is often when we experience our own limitation, when we are extremely compromised in one way or another, and when we feel most disconnected and off our path that we begin to long for a connection with what is limitless and whole.

I think of my own experiences as gateways, unique meetings and blessings, showing up at all the right times. Sometimes it was very easy for me to understand why things were happening the way they were and other times it took me a while to recognize the underlying grace of it all. At this point, I don't view my experiences or anyone else's in terms of good or bad, desirable or undesirable. I feel the most free when I accept life as something ultimately mysterious and wild, like an untouched forest—with fallen trees, big rocks draped in soft moss, little whimsical flowers popping up in some random patches of delicate grass, the fresh smell of soil and pine—all of it so seemingly uncalculated, so quiet and powerful and beautiful.

I don't believe there is anything in anyone's story that needs to be fixed or altered. I would go so far as to say we are not really capable of fixing anything on that level. We can fix a broken chair but not a broken heart. Why? Because the heart was never and will not ever be broken. Our heart is untouchable. It may be, however, that the experiences that are the most outrageous, the events in our lives that are the least comprehensible, the ones that refuse to lend themselves to reason and neat packaging, can become a great motivation to find the door to the vast ocean, the speechless full moon that Rumi talked about. This chapter is about the people and experiences that showed up in the aftermath of some of the most incomprehensible events in my life. In those moments, miraculous events and wonderful people came into my life with perfect timing, showing me new things or old things that I was now receptive to.

These times are the fuel and inspiration behind my ideas about freedom and liberation. They've taught me that love, unconditional love, wherever it comes from, always wins. How it really doesn't matter what happens to us. We don't always need to understand it. We all have the opportunity, at any point of our lives, to listen to our own hearts and allow the love that's inside us to flow through us. The most genuinely difficult times for me were also the most profoundly illuminating. These insights come from deep beyond the surface of things, from seeing up close and personal how convincing darkness, fear, desperation, and loneliness can really be.

No one on this planet has motivated my search for love, and a life that is free and not identified by struggles, more than my oldest daughter Lina. Her smile is one of a few smiles that I have encountered in humans that consistently shows no sign of regret. In spite of her absolutely volcanic disintegration episodes, she is so loving and open-minded. How is this? It's impossible for me to ignore the fact that she has suffered more than almost anyone I know and yet she is so full of light and love. Lina embodies such a powerful paradox. She changed my life. Lina's autism, as recounted in my two previous books about our lives together, *Finding Lina* (2013) and *Beyond Autism* (2019) brought insurmountable struggles: unimaginable nervous system breakdowns, endless seizures, life-threatening car rides, sleep deprivation, deafening screams for help that kept soaring through the air, day after day, night after night. Her difficulties were very slow to subside in spite of the fact that my kitchen became a biomedical and homeopathic laboratory, despite innumerable consultations with shamans, psychics, energy workers, sound therapists, genetic researchers, scientists, neuro movement specialists, inter-relational specialists, anthropologists, neurologists, communication gurus . . . the list never ends. And the consultations continue. Though at this point, at a much slower, more relaxed pace. The ultimate consultation was the one I had with my own inner Spirit. The paradox of Lina, her magic as well as her challenges, was, and is, the ultimate push toward, well, for lack of a word that sufficiently describes this, God. Because somehow, in the middle of all that she went through, grace was always inside her and all around her, holding her hand, holding all of our hands—her little sister's hand, my ex-husband's hand, and mine.

But long before that, when I was a child, I sought the embrace and protection of something I had no name for. I spent much of my childhood roaming alone in the forests and lakes near my home in rural Sweden, connecting quietly with everything around me. And while I certainly didn't have any words to describe this experience, I was reassured by the feeling of being at peace, being one with every tree, every flower, the deep-green, soft moss on the big boulders that were nestled into the hilly landscape, the lakes and the rivers, the valleys and hidden meadows in the middle of forests.

Without anyone asking me to, I chased herds of sheep through hilly woods back to our neighbor's pasture where they wouldn't get into trouble. Without asking anyone's permission, I crawled up on the back of Malin, the fox-brown horse who was perpetually eating too much for her own good with a belly that proved her ongoing indulgences. I loved her so much I just had to climb up on her broad back. They were very short rides and mostly I just sat next to her, staring at her rhythmic chewing of the grass all around the spot where I was sitting. Those times, I was at peace with the universe, without any trace of longing for anything, or anyone, else.

My brothers and I grew up on the campus of a school for adults. Most were high school dropouts who needed a new shot at education, and in many cases life. My father was the headmaster.

There weren't a set of rules spelled out for my siblings about what we could or could not do growing up. Our upbringing was a little bit random, I guess you could say, and some benefits arose from this state of affairs. Staffan, the brother closest to my age—three years older than me—and I habitually swam across the large deep lake near our house and back again after some rest and defrosting on the other side of it. It would take us a couple of hours each way. We did not engage in ideas about the potential dangers of such endeavors. If one of us became tired, the other one would help. If both of us were struggling, the water would save us. It wasn't even discussed. It was just implicit. The sense of freedom and joy that came from being in the middle of that deep, quiet lake became a visceral reminder for me throughout my life of the reservoir always there inside me, regardless of circumstances.

My two older brothers, in their own individual ways, were my co-conspirators early in life. It became increasingly clear to me that life required that I have them.

Per, my oldest brother, had the ability to laugh, with all his might, in the middle of the deepest sorrow. While his brilliant mind and heart was sometimes hidden by the hardships he encountered in his life, Per maintained inside of himself a vision about life, community, happiness and fun that made a permanent impression on me. There were many moments where he was so connected, larger than life, openhearted and incredibly perceptive that I realized that a human being, in connection with the universe, can accomplish anything. As kids, before the more challenging moments of being a teenager and almost adult set in, Per and I were running after and exploring the life of wild rabbits next to the ocean of our summer cottage. Watching those swift little animals I learned that any aspect of our existence on this planet can be wholeheartedly explored and enjoyed; life is full of magic in the moment we devote ourselves to what is right in front of us; in the second we agree to dive into our present life and stay there—absorbed, intrigued, curious, bewildered even, but never bored. Per taught me this. Family life was precarious, riddled with conflict, hidden trauma, and uncontained anxiety. Beyond our immediate family, I often found myself pulled into the lives of very unstable, fearful, and rageful adults who were students at the school where we grew up. While Staffan and I didn't directly discuss our individual experiences within and outside our family, we had some kind of shared understanding that we needed to create an alternative life—a more protected life, with a brighter outlook and less entrenched with trauma and isolation. It had proven to be very important to figure out how to spend time away from the family house, to find words to normalize some of our experiences without getting overwhelmed by fear and disillusionment and to find a way to laugh at some of those compromising situations. Staffan was an expert at finding those words and expressions and this is still one of the main reasons why I never get tired of our regular WhatsApp conversations (he stayed in Sweden, and I moved to the United States). The thing about Staffan and words was, if there wasn't a word for something, he would invent a brand-new one. He would also switch the meanings of words around so that negative words took on positive meanings and positive words could become curse words whenever the situation called for it. There was so much potential and creativity in his language, it seemed like everything was imaginable and constantly changing. In a good way. To me he represented sanity, thoughtfulness, and clarity.

Staffan and I would sprint down the hill from our house to the school kitchen, often in the middle of the night when no one was there. We would find the most exquisite chocolate and vanilla ice cream in the giant freezers down in the basement, get spoons, and sit in the little staff dining-room tucked in right next to the large cooking area while slowly finishing every bit of ice cream that had been packed into large, economy-size containers.

Sometimes in the evening, we would send ourselves to the kitchen to "pick up milk and potatoes." Even those excursions turned into joyous pilfering adventures, which were less about violating boundaries and breaking rules and more about possibility and limitlessness. It was as if the "milk and potatoes," the marathon swims, and our inventive language were the antidotes, the way we showed ourselves that we could make things right, take things back, thrive and find our own remedies regardless of outer circumstances. We could do it our own way, creating joy and opportunity and things to laugh about and look forward to in a world that otherwise appeared mostly gloomy and heavy with premature responsibilities.

Even as a young child, I had a lot of unusual caretaking responsibilities. I was expected or guided (I'm not sure which) to be helpful to the adult students at the school in more serious trouble than myself. They would come to our house when life was tougher than they could handle on their own. Some of them were suicidal, some had substance abuse disorders, some were full of rage and often violent, and some were sexually invasive. I often wondered why they came to our house for help. Both my parents were fighting their own personal battles, while at the same time feeling pressured to hide their private struggles and preserve the public persona of running the school and being people of faith and righteousness. At that time, I hadn't yet developed any of my own problems, and these responsibilities allowed me to rely on something greater than my own fears and inexperience and immaturity. The needs within and outside my family required it. But don't get me wrong; sometimes I was in over my head and very scared. And while I guess you could say that I was quite altruistic, I was definitely not a saint-like child.

When I was very young, I had a childhood friend who had a mother named Eivor, who worked in the school kitchen. I thought Eivor was the closest thing to God in human form. She had four kids and a charismatic, temperamental husband. Eivor was a substantial woman with blondish, grayish hair and green eyes that glittered the way a very still ocean glitters on a late summer afternoon. She had a low-pitched voice and a smile that lit up entire rooms. I loved it when she smiled at me and I followed her around like a dog. I loved her laughter, it was so hearty, appearing to come from deep within her. Though I was a very quiet child, I tried my best to come up with funny, cute things to say to Eivor as often as I could. Eivor was willing to smile and laugh even at bad jokes. Her laughter was just there, constantly waiting deep inside her for the slightest chance to bubble up and flow out into the universe, making everything a little warmer and friendlier. When I was six years old and, I'm assuming, had a bad day, I followed Eivor from the kitchen, while singing out all the Swedish curse words known to man. I sang them, louder and louder, as I walked some twenty yards behind Eivor all the way up the hill to her house. As she disappeared into her house, smiling to herself, I turned around and walked quietly the other way back to my own house. When she reminded me of this story years later, she said she took my curse-singing as a compliment. While I admittedly wasn't very good at following rules, I was an extremely polite child. Eivor knew this and felt that I trusted her so much that I was willing to show her the most unacceptable vocalizations I knew, still somehow sensing that she would love me anyway and that she would understand. She embodied and demonstrated unconditional love for me, and I remember feeling safe and good when she was around.

As my mother's third child, I was often in the way. My mother regularly dropped me off for weeks at a time with a woman named Greta, who lived in the little town about half an hour away from our house. Greta had one daughter, Annelie, who was several years older than I. The older I got, the more I appreciated that Annelie remained a constant in my life. She became my sun. Since Greta had a lot of health issues, and

Annelie loved children, she took me under her wing. She seemed to thrive on making people happy. She loved it when I smiled and laughed, warmed by her light and kindness. Every time I was dropped off at their stone house in the middle of town that looked like a giant square of sugar that had been dipped in green food coloring, I felt that luck had once again returned to my life.

Upon my arrival, Annelie would sit me down by their tiny kitchen table, serving me thick slices of white, sweet bread with generous amounts of soft butter topped with ketchup (yes, you read that correctly) and laid out the options in front of me. We could take her little old white Renault and go swimming in various lakes; we could go get pizza; make popcorn and talk; go check out the mini horses and the parrots and monkeys at the zoo, we could pick some cherries from the tree out in the yard outside their house; or we could go and sit in the living room and talk current affairs with Annelie's mother and her gentle, talkative father, Allan. During their conversation, I would be working on balancing on top of one of the two little round ottomans without legs that one could turn on the side and try to roll forward with. It was one of my favorite things to do. I loved being in there, playing this game of balancing and slowly moving forward on top of the ottoman while listening to Annelie conversing with her parents.

Most days, we ended up doing everything on the list. And when given the option, I always wanted to stay a few more days, basking in the sweetness and joyfulness of my older friend. It was an experience of family, and while not everything was perfect in this family, either, its members were spending time together, sharing a life that to me seemed reassuringly normal, predictable, and protected.

As a young adult, I got a scholarship to work for six months in an orphanage in Junnardeo, a small village in Madya Pradesh, right at the heart of India. There were about forty children, from newborn infants to older kids, in the small, simple building—with no furniture except for the infants' beds—that had become these children's home for various reasons, each more tragic than the next. Three women took care of the children, two of them having suffered abandonment and abuse themselves and with no other place to call home than the very orphanage where they now both lived and worked.

Those six months were so important to me. Not because of anything that I did that was particularly special. I just did what the women showed me to do: feeding and changing babies, playing with the older kids and cooking with the women, trying to be as helpful as I could without being in anyone's way.

With the exception of the main teacher, who knew a few words of English, and who tried without success to teach me Hindu, the women had never seen a white person. The villagers of Junnardeo pointed and laughed at me as I went to the market once a week. They'd never seen someone so pale and strange looking. But when the head doctor who ran the hospital next to the orphanage had first introduced me to the women who worked there, none even raised her eyebrows. From the moment I arrived, they just accepted me. They patiently, gracefully showed me the best they could, without us speaking the same language, how to make chapattis, feed and change as many babies as possible—as quickly as possible—wash the cloth diapers, and help out the older children. Survivors of their own unimaginable trauma, they were still kind and, though pretty firm with the older kids, there was no mistaking their commitment to all the children's' welfare. Since I represented an extra pair of arms and hands that could hold and feed the babies or play with the children, they welcomed me, smiling warmly at all my mistakes and misunderstandings in the kitchen and around the orphanage, patiently integrating me into their lives, stoically, bravely going on living, taking one step in front of the next. They were striking in their ability to take life as it is, do what they could, smile and laugh, open to their lives the way it was, still kind, still beautiful, still full of dignity and integrity and grace. I will never forget those women. They remain my role models and remind me of just how revolutionary unconditional love is.

When I returned to Sweden from India in my early twenties, I spent a few months in my parents' house on the high school campus where I had grown up, before moving to Gothenburg for my university studies. One student, was Sergio. Like many of the students who came to the school, things had not gone well for Sergio before he'd come there, either. He had been born with fetal alcohol syndrome and spent his early years being shipped from foster home to foster home, one situation more detrimental to his well-being and sense of safety than the next. He dropped out of high school and got into drugs and drinking, and he developed a serious sex addiction that made everyday life unbearable.

When we met, he was distracted and hard to connect with at first. But something about his restlessness and isolation reminded me of myself, and soon we became friends. As troubled as he was, Sergio was a gentle, funny person. He made fun of his own sex addiction, my anti-social, hermit tendencies, our unlikely but sweet friendship, and all the funny originals that lived and worked or studied in this strangely intense school environment. One night I had a dream that he and I rolled around in the snow together. It was a dream about innocence, I think. And somehow, that was the most striking characteristic of our friendship.

I baked bread for my friend and we sat together eating and watching silly TV shows in my parents' bed when they were away traveling. Sergio had a reputation of being a womanizer and was a very pretty man but he never did anything more than hug me and kiss my cheeks or my hands. He joked about sitting around in the principal's bed eating homemade bread with the principal's daughter.

Like so many fellow humans, we had both lost our innocence and endured early trauma, and somehow, in the gentleness and respect of our friendship, much of that innocence was restored. On our wandering in the deep, quiet woods around the campus, he sometimes gave me piggyback rides and I felt younger and safer with him than I ever did as a young girl. Sometimes, I would stop by Sergio's room on my way back from a morning swim in the lake for a little extra warmth and cuddles. We never had sex. It was our rule that we would just be friends and not ever make the warmth and the innocence that we had found in each other weird and complex, as it predictably would be if we crossed that line. The school was of a strict Lutheran tradition and the rule was that female and male students weren't allowed in one another's rooms and weren't allowed to engage in sexual relations on campus. One day as I was sitting in Sergio's bed with just my swimsuit on, one of the teachers at the school, let's call him Lasse, was making the rounds of the dormitories to make sure the rules were respected. It was definitely not a good time to try to explain why I was sitting there in that outfit, or, as it were, the lack of one. There was both dismay and amusement in Lasse's face as he wished me good morning.

In a way, Sergio and I were able to turn the narrative on its head. Our childhood traumas were shameful secrets, but now our secrets became about our innocence, and *not* about what everyone assumed it was. It was as if we had a shared opportunity to set things straight for ourselves. The sweetness and innocence of the safe touch that we couldn't have as kids we gave to each other now. And guided by love, we made our own agreement, conducive to the joy and well-being of both of us, deciding together which rules to follow and which ones to break.

Another unexpected source of love and kindness was my friend Mia's mother. She lived by the ocean in a little house with her new boyfriend, in the aftermath of a very shitty divorce. I had met Mia in Gothenburg, where I lived at the time. Mia and I had met waitressing at some catering parties, and ended up running a little café in the middle of the city together. I was very lost. Mia noticed and generously invited me for Christmas with her mother and her mother's boyfriend at their house. There was so much love and freedom and compassion and joy in her mother's house I didn't know what to do with it. I was afraid that my private agony would compromise their holiday. On the night before Christmas I told my friend that I had to leave. She said, "Okay, can you just let my mother know tomorrow morning before you leave?" I was afraid of that but recognized, even in the dull, uncommunicative state that I was in, that it was the honorable thing to do.

As Mia and I walked into the kitchen the next morning, her mother, who had already heard that I had decided to take off, walked up to me, wrapped her arms around me, crying, and shouted in my ears, "*Helena, you* are *not* going *anywhere*! You are staying with us, do you *hear* me!?" She cried and cried and hugged me tight, not showing any signs of letting me go. She just stood there, in the middle of the kitchen, hugging me, crying, and shouting that she was not going to let me leave her house.

It was extremely awkward. And yet, I felt my internal resistance softening. It was impossible not to notice that love was all around me. Bravery. Soldiering. Her outrageous, heartfelt, determined compassion melted my whole body and everything that was in my troubled mind until my resistance to everything that can be good in life dissipated. My choice to leave had been taken away from me, by someone much braver than myself. She took it away from me because she saw that I had no clue what to do with my freedom. So I stayed. I recognized the love. It was the most beautiful Christmas I have ever had. And I understood what grace was, embodied in a middle-aged woman whose heart vibrated for a stranger.

Rascal Flatts performed a song called "God Bless the Broken Road." My youngest daughter, Elsa, and I were driving on a recent sunny late September morning, along a beautiful country road near our farm in North Salem, New York, listening to this song. I told her that while most people may think that this song is about romantic love, to me, it speaks about how our traumas and losses and general hardships can bring us closer to grace inside ourselves. Elsa, pragmatic and perceptive as she is, just shrugged her shoulders as she always does when something is quite obvious to her, and said:

"Well, Mom, that's your interpretation of every song!" And she is right. To me, the most interesting love is the love of grace. The way I see it, our lives offers a series of opportunities to find that one true love. Many of those opportunities appear to be born out of our challenges. There are so many things we consider inconceivable and then they happen and we realize there isn't anything that's too much to endure. The thing that absolutely couldn't happen was the thing that opened our eyes, hearts, and minds and led us toward freedom, openness, and love. It was those challenges, those lost dreams, that confusion and sense of broken-heartedness (though not real) that become like the North Star. And that North Star will lead us home whenever we let it.

I started writing this book as I was approaching menopause. I have lived long enough to know that menopause, ultimately, is a blessing. The hormones involved in this process provide me with the greatest guarantee that I really can't hide and I can't fake it. My hormonal fluctuations keep me honest.

But at the same time I think menopause can become the stuff that happens when we as women take the next step, into our own wisdom, our own harmony, and the way we truly want to be. I had been wary of menopause, seeing women all around me going a little nuts. But by now, I have become more practiced in seeing the opportunity in what is fluctuating and unsettled. I can see that part of the ground I'm standing on is an illusion and nothing much to worry about. I am becoming more deliberate about my own life, how I feel, what I spend my days and nights thinking about, how I begin and end them. I am less afraid of jumping into unknown places. And I don't mean jumping off some bridge because life is unendurable. I'm describing something that feels like jumping straight into the arms of grace, over and over until it seems like the most natural thing to do in life. It seems natural to trust things on this level because I can see more clearly who I really am.

During the worst hours of agony in my adult life, when everything came in like an unstoppable flood, when the devil burst out laughing, I prayed for death. But not in the literal way that I prayed for it in my early twenties. Now, I prayed for the death of separation,

death of fear and blindness, death of stories and negative chatter and self-destructive reasoning, lies and pre-
tense. Death while still here, on this beautiful planet
Earth. Death as liberation, as the most alive, as the
most free and joyful, as what we are meant to be, our
most natural, unconditional state. And as I found that
quiet space in the eye of the tornado, time after time, I
joined the devil and burst out laughing myself. And I
saw the beauty of everything alive. I recognized that all
is good and that all experience is part of the sacred
journey of the life that we came here to live. Am I free?
I say what Stevie Wonder once said, in the introduction
to his stunning music video that illustrates his song
"Free": "A lot of people in this world are not free. I'm
not free, but I'm working on it."

2

Living from the Inside and Some Thoughts about Meditation

The arcane matters
It was beginning to sink in
Those elusive, arcane matters.
I will never find my final destination.
It doesn't exist.
When I saw it for the first time
I thought

something is lost.
Temporary, infinite, constant movement, never-
ending flux.
It was more than I could handle.
It was beyond my vision.
I am not an Eagle! I argued
How will I be able to hold on to anything at all?

One morning when everyone else was sleeping
I was quiet enough to hear
the soft, gentle whisper through the rising sun
explaining my life to me.
You have been given everything.
Your whole life is already here.
You are an Eagle.
You are also earth and sky.
Ocean and Mountain.
All moving things.
And this complete moment,
this in between place,
will never give up on you.
Will constantly, patiently
call your name
until you hear it.

Don't run away
from your temporary place so full of treasures

Don't hide
Don't deny yourself
The moment, and the movement and the flow
that is your life
Claim it
Live it
Laugh and sing it
Dance in that humpty dumpty space
that is your ever evolving universe.
That place where everything grows.
The land between worlds
Where all the beauty in all the universe
Meet up with you and your in-between life.

I worked for decades on other people's freedom, before I realized that all I had to do was to find my own. In the beginning of my work as a psychotherapist in private practice, I did what most psychotherapists do: I tried to figure out what was wrong with my clients. I tried to get to the source of the problem, the core of someone's difficulties. I figured if I only knew what their central pathology was, I would be able to help them. Little did I know that actually, I compounded their challenges. I added more focus to their difficulties and exacerbated their problems. And the process, sure it was interesting, but it was also endless. So eventually I began to understand that their struggle was a kind of illusion; habitual thoughts, running through their minds, triggering a well-known set of emotions, bodily sensations, and reactions, leading to more struggle.

As I got older and wiser I learned not to be so invested in pathology. Without dismissing anyone's difficulties, I gradually learned how to look straight at my own as well as my clients' challenges without being too impressed by them. Without being bogged down by them. Without approaching them with the idea that they needed to be altered, changed, done away with. Eventually, my messages to myself and my clients changed. From trying to figure out what the problem was, I began to move in a different direction. I began talking to myself, my children, my friends, and my clients about our wholeness, our connectedness with everything around us, our light, our desire to love and give and create beauty around us.

"There is nothing wrong with you," I told my clients. "You are just struggling with the way you perceive and relate to yourself." And most of the time, my clients would look at me in disbelief, unable, after so many years of trying to figure out what their problems were, to grasp the idea that there was instead no problem at all. "You don't really need me. I'm not the answer. We can call it a meeting where we discover good things together, but you don't need me for that," I heard myself telling my clients. Those meetings can be done anywhere. There is nothing much to find in our troubled childhoods, in what happened to us, in the cruelty of other people, in our lost marriages, our injured children. These experiences only serve as potential openings to a place that is beyond specifics and free of regret. Liberated of resistance. Beyond the laws of gravity.

The Jamaican Spiritual leader Mooji talks about this state, beyond physical boundaries, limitations, and time. In all of his teachings, poems, and statements, Mooji describes the freedom of the non-dual state of empty and pure consciousness. This, Mooji teaches, is a state where nothing can hurt us, where we have no enemies and where we can discover our eternal, indestructible nature.

Over the years, I began to develop the understanding that while we have our earthly shape, our limited thought pattern, our bodies, our emotions, and our erratic behaviors, we are so much more than that. Beyond it all, we are infinite and unlimited. Beyond our physical form, we are beings of light, connected and inseparable from every bird, every tree, every other human, the sun and the moon, this planet and every other planet. I think it's the interaction between the physical and the infinite that holds the most incredible miracle. And the path toward that interaction, I believe, can be found in the unconditional welcoming of our humanity. Pema Chödrön, in *Wisdom of No Escape*, writes, "The desire to change is fundamentally a form of aggression towards yourself. . . .

Our hang-ups, unfortunately or fortunately, contain our wealth. Our neurosis and our wisdom are made out of the same material. If you throw out your neurosis, you also throw out your wisdom."

The way I look at it, our earthly shape and human tendencies propel us to find our infinite being, our inner light. We will not find it by denying and condemning our humanity. We'll find it by looking straight at our neurotic, obsessive, fearful, grasping, controlling parts, with love. When we relate to our humanness with love, we are in harmony and connecting with our inner light. That love and deep, unconditional acceptance *is* our inner light.

So, who are we? Are we the thoughts that are running through our minds? Are we the feelings that tend to hook up with the thoughts and reinforce whatever it is we're thinking? Are we our experiences? Does our childhood define us? Do our hopes and dreams for the future illustrate who we are? Our birth date? Our marriage? Does our car, our house, our salary, our expertise speak about who we are? What I am about to say may sound absurd coming from someone who has worked as a psychotherapist for as long as I have. Some of my colleagues, reading this, may feel that I am discrediting our profession. And well, yes, they would have a point. Because I don't think any of the above is relevant to who we *truly* are. Ultimately, we are none of those things. Thoughts and feelings come and go. Our past is no more. Our future hasn't happened yet and does not exist. But there is something inside us that always is and always will be. Our true self. A self that isn't personal. Isn't reactive. Cannot be manipulated. Cannot be disappointed or hurt or damaged. The one that watches. The one that stays the same and that is connected with everything and everyone. The pure self, or pure awareness, that doesn't judge, the self that just sees everything, protests nothing, loves everything. Pure being. Infinite being. The undefinable space inside that we can tap into when we allow silence or when we are actively thinking, feeling, and acting in harmony with that love. The infinite presence that we become aware of in the moment we stop letting our past, our personal predicaments, our particular fears and challenges tell us who we are and who we are not and what our lives can and cannot be.

Here, in this harmonious space, is the wordless answer for everything. Here *is* everything. We don't have to imagine it. We don't have to make it up. We don't have to go to therapy to find it. We don't have to travel to see gurus and shamans and astrologers to get there. *We already have it.* We always had it and we always will have it. Our internal being will never die, and will never be impressed by anything, good or bad. For our true self, nothing is preferred or unpreferred. Nothing is chased down or rejected. Everything is beautiful and whole.

And when we connect with this true and eternal part of ourselves, our life starts flowing in a completely different way. Everything becomes so simple. It's almost laughable how simple everything is from this perspective, with this awareness.

Mooji talks about how when a person discovers their inner divine nature, when someone comes home to their "true heart" they become a human being that no longer bothers the world with their anxiety, projections, and judgment. This, Mooji teaches, is what coming off the wheel of samsara is all about. This is were suffering ends and beauty begins.

How did I get to the idea that we are already here, already whole, we are not missing anything, and we don't need to be complemented in any way or fixed or improved? I certainly did not get there through any kind of formal studies. Traditional education is almost invariably focused on becoming something. My most valuable education has very little to do with the letters after my name. My education comes primarily from my life; from observing myself and my clients, from decades of talking with people about their fears, their sadness, and their hopes and triumphs. Good teachers are everywhere, all the time. I found my best teachers in my own life, in my kids, my friends, people on the street. Many of my teachers were animals and birds, particularly the non-domesticated ones. And Lina, my oldest daughter, has been my most striking, shiniest, most undeniable North Star, turning all that I knew upside down. That's what a really good teacher does.

It was only a couple of years into my private practice as a psychoanalyst when she regressed into autism. She was three and a half years old, had her first seizure, lost all of her speech, and propelled into a tornado of sensory disorganization, incontinence, and hyperactivity. In the fifteen years since, she has been an incredible teacher. She is the main reason I have anything to say at all. But what I've learned is not so much *about* her as it is *from* her. I found my most important insights in the life we've shared together. I thought I had to figure out how to make it through, and I learned that making it through isn't necessary. It's perfect the way it is. My daughter has traveled between heaven and hell, high places and low places. It's been my biggest challenge to keep up with her and learn about her experiences. Her language, at this point, is not the language of our frequency. It does appear that she has had a lot of struggle in her life. And yet, there is something about her that is so complete and whole and untouched. The more I learn about and respect the part of her that's totally free and uncompromised—the part that she instinctively recognizes—the easier it is for me to be helpful to her. I can be in the middle of very chaotic situations and offer up a little smile, because I know there is so much more, beyond what I see. I don't need life to incessantly prove itself to me. I have learned to trust that things do work out. Things are not as severe and complicated as we make them out to be.

Over the years, I have come to the understanding that our most natural state is to be happy and free. We don't have to become anything. There is nothing to figure out. If we knew how beautiful and whole we are inside, we would naturally follow some very simple universal guiding principles. But all of it originates from knowing who we truly are. Once we know that we are uncompromised, unaffected, undisturbed, and infinite and that this is the ultimate truth about us, all the comings and goings in life seem less important.

I believe this is true on a personal level as well as in the broader perspective. For example, while we are driven to acts of charity we approach it as something we are doing for someone else. Most of us don't see that we are both the problem and the solution. We are interconnected and no one is somebody else's savior. It's just not that isolated. Every time we try to find the solution on the outside, or think that we are someone else's solution, we get stuck and become ineffective. The former Ethiopian emperor Haile Selassie, in his speech to the UN in 1967, emphasized this in the context of Africa and world politics: "Africa is our nation and is in spiritual and physical bondage because her leaders are turning to outside forces for solutions to African problems when everything Africa needs is within her."

Selassie believed in the possibility of introspection:

We must look into ourselves, into the depth of our souls. We must become something we have never been and for which our education and experience and environment have ill-prepared us. We must become bigger than we have been: more courageous, greater in spirit, larger in outlook. We must become members of a new race, overcoming petty prejudice, owing our ultimate allegiance not to nations but to our fellow men within the human community.

Selassie's view is no less relevant on a personal level— only when we look for the solution within do we have impact on our environment.

"When African righteous people come together, the world will come together. This is our divine destiny."

From this perspective, from the idea that everything comes from inside, how to relate to our life becomes less of a maze, and more just a natural consequence of knowing who we are. When we become secure in the awareness that we are presence, pure awareness, and that our pure being is beyond thoughts and feelings and sensory and physical reactions to all the impermanent phenomena that happens all around us, we start flowing in a very different way. What sent us into a spiral of stress, despair, or even rage now suddenly seems comical. What seemed terrifying in the past, is now more like a benign curiosity. What was tense and cramped and contracted becomes more fluid, gentle, and open. And inside this harmony, with this growing recognition of our own ultimate and infinite power, even very concrete and physical and earthly things begin to work out.

Lina has a book that she used to carry with her when she was younger. It's called *What Is Love?* There are a number of wonderful examples with beautiful colorful illustrations in this book of how love shows up everywhere throughout our daily lives. I think if we look closely, and quiet down sufficiently, we will see that love is in absolutely every little detail of our lives. And that includes us. On my eyeglass case I have taped a little phrase from a fortune cookie that came with my Chinese food long time ago. It says "You don't need love, you *are* the love."

Whether we know it or not, we are so lucky that grace is inside us. It is flowing through us. It *is* us, and we are it. How can we live in the middle of this love and not know it? I don't know.

I do know this. It gets easier when we make less of an effort. We are not getting any closer to our true self by trying to control things. Love doesn't need to be controlled. In fact, love cannot be controlled.

One very simple way to connect with who we truly are is through meditation. Simply sitting down somewhere comfortable and quiet, a little corner of your house or your apartment or your room that you can return to, again and again, day after day, month after month, year after year. You will see, if you haven't already, as the days go by, your life will begin transforming itself in front of your eyes. You return there, maybe early in the morning if possible, setting yourself up for less entangled days. You can light a candle, burn incense, sit in front of a few little things that are dear to you—some pictures of your children, some beautiful stones or seashells, a feather, your deceased mother's necklace, a couple of flowers in a little vase, a piece of driftwood that you found during a time that illuminated something important to you—whatever it is that reminds you of your intention to connect with your higher ground, your pure presence, your heaven on earth.

In this place that you just keep returning to, faithful to your intention of finding out the truth about yourself, committed to your own happiness and freedom, you can allow your thoughts, feelings, sensations, and impressions to come and go without trying to restrict or chase after them. If you are new to meditation, you can begin by sitting for just a few minutes. Just sit in that space that you prepared for yourself, with the intention of making a brief introduction of yourself to yourself. No need to overdo it. No need to get into struggles between states of thinking and not thinking. All is good. The thoughts are good. The space in between them is good. It's all sacred. The upheaval and the calm. No reason to start glorifying one state and condemning another.

Simply breathing naturally, in and out, letting everything be, allowing life to come and go in a rhythmic, spontaneous way that is not the product of agendas, manipulations, and strong opinions. To slowly notice that for a few seconds, there is a space that's not filled up with a thought. And then, just allowing thoughts and impressions to come and to go, gradually fading away into the periphery, replaced almost miraculously by space and calm silence, a sense of entering unclaimed territory, a little meadow in the middle of the forest. And, in the middle of that space, so full of possibility and a kind of spontaneous, undefined joy, something else—a sense of well-being, of connection, a feeling of non-entangled love, a peacefulness, something open and free. A few seconds of that, then a thought, maybe leading to another thought, maybe to something that's more of an internal discussion. Maybe you can let yourself notice how that internal discussion begins to fire up, gain momentum, speed up the heart rate, and quicken your breathing again. Maybe you can let yourself be okay with that. Seeing it, without letting it discourage you and then letting it subside again. Finding that increasing spaciousness again, a little quicker this time, noticing how it's always there, waiting for you to let yourself come back to it. Seeing, with fascination and awe, how, as soon as the thoughts subside, the second it happens, that free space just keeps popping back in.

For me, the best and easiest time to do this is first thing in the morning. Before my kids and my dog wake up, before I respond to texts and emails, before I get busy in my own head and get into the things that I need to do that day. I light a candle and some incense in a little corner of my home office. I sit down, close my eyes, breathe in, breathe out, naturally and without trying to control anything. I sit there, allowing everything to be what it is. Slowly, the silence and vastness inside comes to the surface. I notice my thoughts and how I sometimes try to catch one of them or figure something out. I may sit there and fix the hole in the fence or water the plants in the garden or order something on Amazon. As soon as I notice what I'm doing, I let it drift away again. I don't push it away. I don't condemn it. I may even smile internally at it. I don't give myself a lecture about being terrible at meditating. I just let it drift.

A soft, gentle vibration may begin to make itself known around my face, arms and hands, spine, neck, heart space, wherever it wants to go, different each time. The silence begins to feel peaceful. No longer feeling the need to go after anything, I begin to sink into the vastness, the peace, the well-being of it all, and while nothing seems particularly important, everything seems quite possible. Sometimes a very direct, clear thought comes to me as I'm sitting there. An idea that's free of anxiety and effort, an impulse that feels like a kind of deep intuition about something. I notice that and go back to the quiet. Sometimes I sit there for half an hour, sometimes an hour, other times fifteen or twenty minutes. The length of it is not important. The important thing is that it works. What I most value about meditation is that it's shown me that there is something inside me that never changes and always responds to me, welcomes me, whenever I stop trying and start to listen.

Rumi, in his poem "Wax," describes searching for something that is already there and does not need to be found. "I must have been incredibly simple or drunk or insane" he writes, "to sneak into my own house and steal money, / To climb over my own fence and take my own vegetables." In this poem, the search for solutions ends and awareness comes the moment we recognize that the answer is beyond our questions and opinions. We won't find the answers through searching and struggling and trying to hold on, but in our allowing and recognizing the the breath of life that pulsates through us, that is inside of us, is us.

3

Loving What Is—An Openhearted Approach

This is a wonderful day. I've never seen this one before.

—Maya Angelou

I love you
Child, stranger, ex-husband, life, lover, leaf,
worm, coffee stain on my shirt
Without condition
Fear, agenda, and fake agreements

are not surviving these tornadoes.
I am you
We walk sweat cry laugh
We argue and we reconcile
We dig deep holes for ourselves and each other
and climb ladders that reach heaven
We fly!
we crawl
we take big bold brave leaps
into uncharted territories
We see everything, finally!
But finally disappears
And we are back to blind, fumbling, losing,
grasping,
blushing even, since we didn't have the capacity to
shred our human skin
or our despicable egos.
Something, in fact, gently encouraged us to live there
in the middle of paradox and confusion
Unimpressed by the deep pot-holes on our path.
We may not quite know our way out of some
dark cages
But we have not forgotten the sun
And the sun has not forgotten us
We are still here and the sun is still here
There is a river and an open field and a breathtaking view on top of a majestic mountain

We laugh as we stretch our wings and let go
We sigh as we float on the most gigantic sea turtle
across the glittering ocean
Love is above and below us
Surrounding us, reminding us
To remember what we know and take our next
breath

If we have a mission as humans, I think it's much simpler than we imagine. I think we are asked, or rather, we asked ourselves, to be here, fully, in our physical shape, wholeheartedly human, while at the same time aware and connected with our infinite self, our inner being. And when we open up to the fact that our infinite self is not opposed to our humanity, as we learn there doesn't have to be a war going on between our humanity and our inner, sacred self, we can begin to relax. We can realize, supported by our infinite self, that there is nothing in particular to hold on to about our humanity, nothing to fix or improve. We are here to learn about what's real and what is not real, what is timeless and temporary. We are here to allow ourselves to be connected both to the physical and the spiritual world.

When and if we learn to develop this ability to enjoy our humanity while at the same time live in awareness of our infinite nature, our lives become less static and serious and more fluid and playful. We can begin to welcome everything, all the time, allowing it to flow through us, like a river, sometimes wild and furious, sometimes quiet and peaceful, all of it illuminating where to go next and how to do everything with a soft, open heart. Pema Chödrön, on meditation, in her book *When Things Fall Apart*, writes:

> *We can be with what's happening and not dissociate. Awakening is found in our pleasure and our pain, our confusion and our wisdom, available in each moment of our weird, unfathomable, ordinary everyday lives.*

Whether we are meditators or not, we all have opportunities to see that everything that comes into our life is here to teach us and help us and take us toward our own inner light. We don't have to distinguish between bad experiences and good ones. There is no such thing as useless, wasted time, and we are not here to find escape routes from our reality. When we welcome our lives, ourselves, and each other, without objecting and rejecting and resenting and trying to control things, we begin to see the beauty in everything. That beauty is very real. It can become increasingly prominent in our awareness. When we open our heart to our life the way it is in this moment, we cannot help but love it. And we find ourselves appreciating everything.

This sense of deep appreciation for every little detail of our lives is extremely powerful. If we were to start every day by thinking about all the little things that miraculously are working out all the time, the things that taste really good, the way the sun warms our faces, the calmness and sincerity of the cloudy days, the comfort of our soft beds, the incredible Irish butter that is melting on our warm toast, the invigorating coffee, the delicious little well-being sounds the dog makes and the gentleness in her eyes, the car that drives us where we need to go, most of the time, the fresh-tasting toothpaste . . . you get the idea. The list is as limitless as our lives. The more we tune into all those incredible details the more we see the bigger miracles. And when we appreciate our lives and each other in it, we become aware of an underlying joy, a sense of well-being and soft vibration in our heart space, a sense of possibility and adventure—it all just grows and grows until we can look at ourselves in the mirror and see only beauty and possibility.

Mooji describes the power of gratitude and how when we say thank you to life, to God, to our innermost being, even if we don't know what we are grateful for, but willing to say thank you anyway, our vibration changes. We feel light and loving and open. We see the goodness of everything. We stop worrying about things. We begin to tune into universal truth.

Relating to our lives in this way makes everything appear sacred. Whatever comes into our lives and everything that fades out of it, the highs and the lows, the triumphs and the disappointments—it's all love, and sacred, and here to make us aware that we are already home.

In the summer of 2019, my ex-husband and I took our children Lina and Elsa to the Bahamas for a week of craniosacral treatments and dolphin therapy for the family. The dolphins' vocalizations produce sound waves that create alternating regions of compression and expansion that form small bubbles in the cell membranes. These bubbles assist in the transport of important neurological molecules from outside to inside neurons. The idea is that the dolphin's sound frequencies can modify the human brainwave activity. EEG tests of brain frequencies in individuals who just experienced these dolphin sounds have showed a dramatic shift into much more relaxed, connected states. Those very particular sound waves that dolphins make helps human brain waves shift from high frequency beta waves that are associated with concentration, alertness, but also worry and anger, to low-frequency alpha (relaxation, creativity, calm) and even theta waves (intuition and a sense of connectedness with others).

It is also believed that dolphin therapy can stimulate a kind of synchronization that improves the communication between left and right hemispheres in a person. While making the various sounds that produce these beneficial frequencies, the dolphins carefully touch their human clients. It was an amazing sensation to have these large, gentle animals touch us, mostly on various spots of our heads as we floated on our backs in the water with a craniosacral therapist holding onto our feet.

As I was laying there in the water, floating in that dreamlike state where everything seemed possible, feeling the love and power of the dolphin around me, I had a strong wish to stay with them. I wanted to live as a dolphin, doing what they were doing, learn to make their sounds, flow and vibrate together with them. The moment I registered that thought the dolphin pushed my forehead deep down under the water until I started choking. With water in my nose and throat, I came back to the surface, coughing and gasping for air. So much for living the rest of my life as a dolphin. I laughed at myself and blessed the dolphin for reminding me in her own way that I have to be where I am, present and open to my own life, without regret and willing to love it and see its beauty. I climbed out of the pool with an open heart and a sense of being in complete harmony with everything alive. Nothing seemed complicated or unattainable. I had a sense of life's perfection. My own, Lina's, Elsa's, my ex-husband's. I was in sync with my universe and I felt free to live my life in exactly the way I wanted to. The dolphins had reminded me of what had been there all along.

How can we learn how to trust and love ourselves and our lives the way they are? How can we relate to our lives unconditionally? Become aware of the beauty of it all? Many people, when going to therapy or taking a meditation class or hooking up with a life coach or reading a self-help book, do so with the intention of changing something about themselves or someone else around them. But I believe the results would be much more convincing if the intention was focused on finding that one does not need to change within oneself. Albert Einstein, in spite of many early and later personal challenges, became one of the greatest scientists of the twentieth century, revolutionizing math and science with his theory of relativity and quantum physics, and in his essay, "This I Believe" In a 1950 essay read for a broadcast series called *"This I Believe,"* Einstein wrote:

The most beautiful thing we can experience is the Mysterious—the knowledge of the existence of something unfathomable to us, the manifestation or the most profound reason coupled with the most brilliant beauty. . . . I am satisfied with the mystery of life's eternity and with the awareness of—and glimpse into—the marvelous construction of the existing world . . . it appears to me that the most important function of art and science is to awaken this feeling among the receptive and keep it alive.

Einstein understood that happiness comes from the inside and from loving what is. While eventually receiving external rewards for his work, including the Nobel Prize in Physics in 1921, his earlier life involved many hurdles and not much recognition. But Einstein was intrinsically motivated.

"I am happy," he wrote, "because I want nothing from anyone. I do not care about money. Decorations, titles or distinctions mean nothing to me. I do not crave praise. I claim credit for nothing. A happy man is too satisfied with the present to dwell too much on the future."

Einstein's unstoppable and joyous creativity was founded on his ability to love what is. He sensed his own internal power and had an intuitive awareness of how the most brilliant beauty, the mystery of life's eternity, had something to do with him and his ability to create. And however astoundingly his brain worked, Einstein realized that solutions and inspiration were not to be found in thinking harder about something but rather in slowing down, enjoying life, and opening up to something beyond his own thought process:

"I think 99 times and find nothing. I stop thinking, swim in silence, and the truth comes to me."

It may seem simple, but most people struggle in this area. We have trouble slowing down enough to allow who we are to come to the forefront of our awareness. We can't learn about who we are while simultaneously running around trying to alter ourselves. In such a state of fixing and reconstructing, we cannot discover our own inner being. And because we think that life becomes only as good as what is happening or not happening to us, most of us spend a whole lifetime in fear—fear or losing, fear of wanting, fear of not getting, fear of not being enough, fear of being too much, fear of seeing and finding what we don't feel ready to see and find, fear of being alone with ourselves . . . the list goes on. If we stay there, no tranquilizers, no drugs, no alcohol, no yoga retreat, no job, no lover, no husband or wife or child or good friend, no amount of money, nothing, can make up for, compensate or console us.

But thankfully, we have another option. We can welcome everything in our lives. The comings and goings of things. The ebb and the flow. We can get immersed in every little second of our present moment and see the beauty of everything we experience. That's a much easier option, much more joyful and free than running, fighting, regretting, and repairing. The problem with trying to fix what we consider broken, is that it will be an unending marathon. The harder we try, the more we run, in fact, the more whatever we are running from, comes after us.

Have you ever experienced this phenomenon: When you are no longer afraid of something, it stops happening? When I first came to New York City in the early

1990s, a friend came to visit. I rode the subway all the time and never had any problems or second thoughts about it. My friend, however, was very uncomfortable in the subway system, afraid to be attacked, robbed, and accosted by dangerous people. So we walked to get where we were going during her visit. At one point, however, we were both so tired that we decided to make an exception and take the subway back to my apartment. As soon as we got down to the track where the platform was, a man approached us in an aggressive, threatening manner. I don't think it was a random coincidence. My friend is intuitive and felt his aggression even before he expressed it. While I don't ultimately believe anyone wants to be either afraid or aggressive, the expectations of my friend and this man's aggression pulled them toward each other. My friend was afraid, and fear is not only contagious but also invites the very thing we are afraid of. What we are focused on becomes what it is.

We are here to learn about our own influence on our own lives. We are here to learn how to trust that our universe is benevolent and we have endless opportunities to learn how to create lives that we are happy to have. We are here to learn from our own creations and get increasingly intentional about how we create.

When we let go of our fears, we no longer need to fantasize about paradise at some remote point in our future lives or afterlife. Without fear, without regretting and grasping, dreading and begrudging, we find that we don't have to wait for something amazing to happen, or for our afterlife; we are already in paradise here on earth. We know the truth. We know that all is well and that we are always protected and loved. The second little story in "Six Little Stories with Lots of Meaning" (source unknown) is about babies. "When you throw babies in the air, they laugh because they know you will catch them. That is trust."

As we get older, our instinctual response is very often to run from our fears, run as fast as we can, and hope that it won't catch us. We shut down in the face of what we are afraid of. We tighten instead of softening. We may try to reason with our fear. Plead and beg and even threaten it. But have you noticed, none of that is particularly effective when it comes to fear? The more we engage with it, the more it becomes part of our lives.

Addiction of any kind is one way of trying to figure out fear and anxiety and other difficult experiences, emotions, and sensations. And, let's face it, it does work for some time. But whatever relief we experience from pills, alcohol, sex, carbs, money, or codependency is fleeting. The anxiety returns with a vengeance as soon as the effect of our particular drug subsides. We are caught in a vicious cycle of feeding an insatiable monster that grows bigger and bigger after every feeding. We become so focused on the very fear or distress or despair that we're trying so desperately to avoid that our whole life fills up with it. Only when we step out of this unsustainable race to feel better, experience instant gratification or pleasure, can we notice that those attempts to manage things, however feeble, are sacred too. The times we spend away from the truth show us what is real and what isn't. It's almost as if we have to get lost before we can find our way home. We have to experience the difference between confusion and clarity, between being alienated from ourselves and others and truly at home with ourselves and our universe. It is almost as if the remedy is in the space between being lost and being found.

There was a time in the history of mankind when running away from things was a really good idea. If a tiger or a bear came our way, running might have been our best option. But where are the tigers and bears now? Many of us don't even have to worry about having food and shelter. But we still have anxiety. We've just replaced the source of it. We fear getting older, being left behind, being alone, being humiliated, abandoned, overwhelmed, sick, dying. We fear that others will let us down, or that we will let them down, or that we will let ourselves down or that they will let themselves down. We are afraid of not having what we need or having too much, we are afraid of being happy and afraid of being sad. And most of all, we are afraid of being afraid.

In the poem "A Community of the Spirit," Rumi encourages the reader to quiet down, listen to something other than our own fears and allow good things to happen. "Open your hands," he writes, "if you want to be held. / Why do you stay in prison," he asks, "when the door is so wide open?"

How do we open our hands? How can we learn to trust the goodness of our lives? How can we go beyond our story and stay in silence with whatever experience we have at any given moment, without trying to alter, improve, polish, or exacerbate it? How do we learn to trust that all of it is temporary and stop giving it so much of our obsessive attention? How can we begin to say yes to whatever is, knowing it's not as big a deal as it seems and it won't stay like that forever? How can we be here, with whatever our life is in this very moment, allowing it to make us softer, more open, and receptive? How can we learn to focus on the beauty of our universe? And how can we keep our joyfulness and trust in the midst of challenge? Contemporary Swedish singer/songwriter Lisa Ekdahl wrote a song called "Jag Tar Vara på Vattnet Då Åskan Går" (I collect the water when it's thundering). This rare and beautiful love song to earth and spirit illustrates a willingness to live wholeheartedly through everything. It describes an openness and a trust, a kind of versatility that goes in every direction, supporting the whole. She finds an ally in "the black soil," in "everything that grows." In spite of hardship, she celebrates "the seed that is busting out of its hard shell," trusting everything that happens, making "a pact with the nameless God."

So if we are hardwired to flee danger, most of us have an inclination to bolt. But we no longer need that burst of adrenaline. Or those ancient strategies. Escape routes. Plans of attack. Today most of us need the opposite. We need to learn how to stay. To soften. To put our defensive weapons down. To be in silence and do nothing. To play more and trust more and let love bring us home to ourselves.

I find that teachers of that love and patience, of gentleness and non-defensiveness, are all around us, often showing up out of nowhere, when we least expect it, in the most unlikely places. They are the real superheroes, preserving peace and sanity through their kindness.

He was a cabdriver. Other than his name, Seine, and his gentle, brown eyes, I knew very little about him. He drove me and Lina home one night when we were still living on the Upper West Side in New York City. Lina has always enjoyed car rides. When she was younger, she was even more passionate about them. Getting out of cars, cabs, buses, and trains was not always as easy as getting into them. In the midst of trying to make a smooth exit from the cab that night, a bundle of things—gift certificates, personal documents such as my driving license, a blank check, cash—fell out of the little red bag

I carried those important items in. As bedtime ceremonies were finally coming closer to an end, my doorbell rang. It was Seine. He looked at me with his gentle brown eyes and without dramatic gestures and overtures, he just said, "Your things," and handed me my red bag.

Seine got a finder's fee and a big hug, none of which he knew what to do with. More than that, he got my attention. I will never forget his gentle and kind, matter-of-fact conscientiousness. He was no longer just one of the (at the time) fifty thousand cabdrivers in New York City. He was a man who opened his heart to a stranger. A person with integrity and compassion. A quiet superhero.

He struck me as someone who lived at peace with himself. Who had found clarity about who he wanted to be and who lived in harmony with the universe and himself. Though driving a cab in New York City has got to be one of the most stressful endeavors one can possibly take part in, he was there, doing his work with grace, showing no regret or bitterness, treating his passengers with love and compassion. As Seine left to go back to his cab, I thought, "He must really like himself. He seems to have so few regrets about anything—he must really have figured out a thing or two about self-acceptance."

In all of her books, Buddhist nun Pema Chödrön talks about staying with what is. Simply staying, without trying to alter or improve, without having to deny or defend or rationalize or justify. In *Taking a Leap*, Chödrön writes:

> *We start by making friends with our experience and develop warmth for our good old selves. . . . This leads to trusting that we have the strength and good-heartedness to live in this precious world, despite its land mines, with dignity and kindness. With this kind of confidence, connecting with others comes more easily, because what is there to fear when we have stayed with ourselves through thick and thin.*

Allowing ourselves to live our lives in a more kind, light-hearted, and fluid way, where thoughts, feelings, things, people, and experiences come and go, brings vitality to our lives. If we approach life with some degree of play-fulness, discriminating a little less between good experiences and behavior and bad ones, letting all of it flow through us and teach us and show us and enliven us, we begin to foster a kind of independence in our relationship with what is going on around us. We may realize that we don't have to make up elaborate stories about every little and big challenge that occurs in our lives. We can see it, allow it, accept it, appreciate it, and move on, trusting that all of it, if we don't declare war on it, will bring us closer to who we are, to our true nature. We can look at ourselves with a little more love and gentleness.

We can remind ourselves that we are here trying to learn how to open our hearts to ourselves and one another, to breathe more fully and approach our physical as well as our spiritual self with joyful curiosity.

Have you ever seen a little kitten watching her own paws? Suddenly, her eyes widen as she notices that she had not just two, but four paws. Wow. She stares and stares, joyfully engaging in the expanding miracle of her incredible little body. It is pure awe. Pure awareness. Pure presence. Absolutely nothing is lacking, there is just the overwhelming curiosity and joy over the second set of paws.

The idea is to take what you love and feel good about and milk it. When something makes you smile, when you have a really exquisite joke that makes you and everyone around you laugh, you just know, instinctually, that this joke, this laugh, this good moment will make everything in your world better, brighter, more fun and more joyous. You find yourself in the right vibration, and now everything seems much less important and also, at the same time, more doable. Not just the thing you laughed about, but everything. Your fear and regret seems so far away. Everything you want suddenly seem so doable. And it's not just what it seems like, it's what it is. You are in the frequency of expansiveness. You are lined up with everything that makes you smile, and as you line up with it, without being overinvested and obsessive about what you want or don't want, it is indeed coming closer to you.

American poet Mary Oliver, who really did figure out a thing or two about being open to the ever-present miracle of life, once said: "Listen, are you breathing just a little, and calling it a life?" How much can be contained in a little short sentence! I am not exactly sure what Mary Oliver had in mind when she said this. But her words remind me of how reconnecting with our full breath helps us relate to our own humanity, our thoughts, our feelings, our personality, our temperament, in a much more proportional way. Our full breath, free of objection, resentment, regret, fear etc. hooks us right up with an awareness of our own inner being. And connected with the vast, the pure awareness inside ourselves, we learn how to look at ourselves in a more lighthearted way. As we find ways to relate to our humanity in a loving, appreciative, openhearted way, we are in harmony with the way that the much larger part of ourselves—call it grace, God, our inner being, God-self, source, or call it nothing at all—relates to us.

When we think kind thoughts, when we treat ourselves gently and with respect, we are in harmony with the innermost part of ourselves. Everything seems possible. Everything makes sense. Everything is beautiful and whole. We are no longer in conflict with what is ultimately true about us. When we relate to ourselves in the opposite way, with regret, doubt, accusation and even hatred, we quickly become tense, contracted, rocky, miserable.

Sometimes, this lack of faith in oneself and one's life is so intense that it cannot be processed as something inside a person. In such cases, it is projected onto something or someone else. One ongoing example of such self-hatred, with the most extreme historical as well as current consequences, is racism. I believe that racism is an attempt to try to escape from misguided beliefs about oneself, an intolerance of oneself that is so powerful that it cannot be observed by the person as something within him or herself. Subsequently, the person experiences it through someone on the outside. No one who truly loves and accepts themselves can simultaneously be a racist, or a hater of any kind. We have a lot of challenge in the area of self-love, self-acceptance, and self-compassion and because that is so we spend a lot of time running and hiding from the negative things we perceive in ourselves and projecting them onto others around us.

From the time of my training to become a psychotherapist, for quite a number of years, I had the pleasure of working with an African American man who was diagnosed with transient psychotic features. Early on in our work together, it became clear that my client sincerely believed that I was black too. At the time, I saw his interpretation of me as black as his way to ensure his own safety and comfort in a racist world. He was stuck with me as his therapist, and he did what he had to do. Because, if I was white, how could I possibly understand him? If I was white, how could he open up to me?

But also, I think we have good reason to question Western society's traditional view of knowledge. In my own view, the one who knows isn't necessarily the one with the most education, material success, prestige, or even mental stability. Clarity and insight don't always originate from the most organized, tidiest, most esteemed places. I have learned my fullest, most important lessons from myself about life and living in times of dark, terrifying, boundaryless, prestige-less places. I have received wisdom from others in the most profound ways, when their whole world was in shambles; while the world around them said they were just dysfunctional and damaged. I think now, my client was seeing something in me that most people couldn't. The hardship this man had experienced in his life, had, in some ways, created a kind of openness in his thinking that allowed him to become more creative in ways that were actually, ultimately, supportive to him. He found a way to let me be a part of his life. It was his receptivity, rather than anything that I did as a therapist, that somehow allowed him to engage deeply with me and talk about his life in a truly openhearted way. I was so happy and grateful for his trust. He saw something that someone else hadn't lived enough life to perceive. I will clarify this further in a later chapter about Mehari, an African man who, while he was not my biological father, became a father figure to me in every other sense of the word, representing safety, hope, and a bright vision for the future. But the important thing about my client was that he somehow, in spite of the fact that his life in many ways bore glaring witness to the oppression that he had lived through for all of his life and that marked him so deeply, he had the courage and the heart to stand above all that and allow me into his life. And I believe that I learned much more from him than he ever did from me.

A couple of years ago, I had the pleasure of watching *The Journey of Man: A Genetic Odyssey*, a documentary built on the book with the same title, written in 2002 by Spencer Wells, an American geneticist and anthropologist. Wells used theories and techniques of genetics and evolutionary biology to trace the origin of humankind. Through his research, Wells was able to trace humanity at its earliest origin, proving that all human beings descend from one single man who lived in Africa about sixty thousand years ago. Wells believes that the San people, a group of Africans that currently lives in a western part of southern Africa, are the modern-day direct descendants of our earliest ancestors. Skin color, hair, height, and body type, Wells declares, are nothing but the human adjustment to variations in climate. It's yet another astonishing example of our bodies' genius way of adjusting and surviving various conditions. Ultimately, this is further proof, not of our differences but of our similarities, our oneness, and how natural it would be for us to love each other. It could become powerful reasons for us to love and honor every one of our differences and every one of our similarities, all showing us how adaptable and ingenious life is.

When author and poet Maya Angelou was working on the 1993 film *Poetic Justice* (as recounted in an interview with George Stroumboulopoulos, aired on a New Year's Eve episode on Tuesday December 31, on CBC), she watched two men on the set arguing with each other. She walked up to them, tapped one of them on the shoulder, and said, "May I speak to you?" The man wouldn't listen and kept up his argument. It became increasingly heated. The young man dismissed her, "Do you know how blah blah blah, I don't give a . . . !" "Yes, I know," Angelou responded, "however, let me speak to you. When was the last time anyone told you how important you are? Did you know our people stood on auction blocks, were sold, bought and sold, so that you could stay alive today?" The man, whose name, unbeknownst to Dr. Angelou, was Tupac Shakur, finally heard her and started to weep. It was a life-altering moment for Shakur. He recognized the responsibility he had toward his ancestors. How whatever they had endured and survived before him had allowed him the life he currently had. And in that moment, he saw clearly how he had the choice in his own life to shut down and fight it or open up and welcome it.

This lesson, of course, is not just for Shakur. It's for all of us. We are all the offspring of those first, brave, and resilient Africans, whose survival instincts and ingenuity gave us our lives. We all benefit from those who came before us, whose struggles and lives gave us our chance to exist on this beautiful planet, to love ourselves and one another, to find our happiness and to pass it on. Our early ancestors were brave and creative, and their courage made it possible for us to have a life, to live, breathe, love, and learn.

Our fear of loving wholeheartedly and unconditionally is powerfully illustrated in the area of romantic love. I think it is safe to say that we are often very limited in our views of how we can express this kind of love. I believe fear and ignorance about who we truly are is the main reason for most disconnectedness as well as overinvolvement in relationships with others. We put the cart before the horse. It is not, and will never be, about finding the perfect partner. Everything starts inside. Everything is born out of our connection with ourselves. When we are in harmony with ourselves, we see and experience harmony all around us. There is nothing to figure out on the outside. No one to fix. No one to convince or win over or manipulate or improve or repair. When we figure out how to love ourselves, how to be in true peace with ourselves, how to appreciate ourselves, how to feel joyous and loving inside ourselves, everything around us, outside us, is instantly upgraded.

In Western cultures, men more than women seem to be limited by fears of being overwhelmed and captured and stifled by another person. Many women express fear of not being sufficient in themselves and having to find a man to complement them. We forget that no one on the outside can change how we feel inside. We don't have to live up to anyone else's expectation. All we have to do to create harmonious, loving, playful, pleasing relationships with others is to find that way of relating to ourselves.

Force never works. Conditions, threats, ultimatums, regrets, resentments, desperation, manipulation—all are just misguided ways of trying to compensate for the fact that we have strayed away from our truest inner being, our inner pure love, that doesn't regret or resent anything about us and our lives. When we are in sync with ourselves, awake and connected with our inner being, our inner light, we have no need to change or boss around or regret and resent or avoid others. All of our relating to others starts to flow in an entirely different way. We suddenly find all kinds of reasons to enjoy and appreciate the people in our lives. It is easy for us to remember why we love them. At the same time, when we are connected with ourselves in this way, always focused on staying in harmony with our inner being, our inner light, what other people do and don't do, who they are and who they are not, become less important. When we learn to experience ourselves through the eyes of grace, our relationship with others is automatically enhanced.

Mooji talks about how true love, while the shape of it changes, never leaves us. He describes how this love, the love that "simply blossoms inside the heart and gives light to the world," has nothing to do with effort or fantasy but becomes apparent when we recognize unity rather than duality, when we get quiet enough to connect with our own inner pure Being; our own sacred divinity.

Many relationships—marriages, partnerships, parent-child constellations, work relationships, even friendships—are based on trying to modify each other's behaviors, feelings, moods, and motivations. If all the energy spent on trying to change each other was focused on connecting with who we really are, internally, our relationships would revolutionize. Divorce lawyers would run out of clients. Marriage has become such an immensely complex institution. The focus, I believe, is misguided. No one should have to shoulder the responsibility of making someone else happy. It's a truly impossible mission. That basic assumption that someone else is responsible, someone else has the solution, the remedy, the love that we need, is faulty. It focuses on the wrong relationship. The only relationship that can make things right is our own relationship with ourselves. And yet, we keep trying to find the answer in each other rather than within ourselves.

Marriage is certainly not always, or even commonly, a happy institution. A lot of married people find themselves in marriages that have become less and less intimate as the years go by. Dissatisfaction grows, and communication shuts down. It's not for lack of trying. There are endless sacrifices, caring for kids and partners and ignoring oneself, putting up with soulless interactions, working, cleaning, and getting mad.

Women are often particularly oblivious to caring for themselves. So many women are perpetually dissatisfied in their marriages. Everyone knows someone who is not just in an unsatisfying marriage but in an outright miserable one. It is that basic misunderstanding underlying so many unhappy agreements. The idea that somehow, the marriage, the relationship, the other, the stuff outside ourselves, is where the solution and the work is. If we can figure out how to make our partner better, understand us more, be more attentive, receptive, willing, and mutual, all will be good. It's so natural for us to go there. And so utterly ineffective. And the misery isn't really in what someone else is doing to us. The misery is in our reaction to it, our unreasonable expectations of our loved ones, our feeling of powerlessness when we are trying to change what we have no control over.

One of my close friends has figured out a lot of things about well-being, living creatively, and not allowing things on the outside to stop the natural and inspiring progression of her own life. Her husband is a passionate painter, quite the personality, not easy to live with and extremely focused and obsessive about his art. By most standards, life with him is very difficult. The only reason they are still together is that she, somehow, still loves him and she has always had pretty good boundaries in terms of what she can and cannot do. For the most part, she focuses on herself, her life, and the things she enjoys doing and that bring her satisfaction. Somehow, that allows her to still love this man. The fact that she knows how to pay attention to herself and love herself enough to assert some space for herself is what saves her love for him. She is not easily victimized. I don't know where my beautiful friend will go with this. But I do have a feeling it will all work out for her, whether she stays in this marriage or moves on from it.

This is, of course, not to say that one should uphold a marriage or a commitment to a friend or any kind of relationship regardless of its challenges. There is a time to stay and a time to leave. Whether one stays in a difficult relationship or decides to leave it, or simply let it fade away naturally, or improve naturally, there is much less work to do on the outside in any kind of interaction and everything to win from simply listening to one's own heart. Because here everything, regardless of circumstances, is already good. The funny thing about this, I have found, is that when we are tuned into our inner being, nothing on the outside is all that important. We are in an unconditional state. Truly free and open. And while it no longer seems as important to us what happens, others are going to respond positively to our upgraded vibration. Someone else will be drawn into our universe, reflecting where we are with ourselves.

And the universe is not stingy or punitive, affording us just one or two chances to find insight. The universe gives us endless opportunities and ongoing, never-ending chances to allow such opportunities into our lives. The universe is generous and large, full of incredible surprises and blessings. All we have to do is to quiet down, look beyond our fears, and trust the love that never left us.

It's undeniable that for many, *not* focusing on our worst fears in relationships can be really challenging. Many women and men have experienced violations in the realm of physical and romantic love. The memory of it may be so intense that closeness with another will trigger associations back to the original trauma. This kind of trauma often comes with the experience of powerlessness, of not being able to prevent someone from taking something that is ours; something as sacred as our innocence and trust. We can get stuck in that feeling of being involuntarily invaded and not able to stop it. In the name of trying to protect ourselves, we can spend years and decades depriving ourselves of something that can be an incredibly beautiful, connected, and joyful part of our lives. What is the turning point? How do we heal from various forms of abuse? How do you learn to accept yourself as a whole and free being again?

Most importantly, the solution is not on the outside. The answer lies within, in knowing who we are, and in learning to live in harmony with that awareness rather than in slavery to forces outside ourselves. But it is the strong past experiences of powerlessness that give us the biggest incentive to want to find a way to live nurtured, protected, and enlightened by our own inner being. If we truly want to be free, and if we are serious about wanting to be happy, we will learn that this inner light never went out. That ultimately, we were never compromised.

Some people would protest and claim that the assertion that we weren't compromised is a form of denial of experiences too difficult to process. I would say that the awareness of who we truly are gives us a perspective that we had trouble holding onto in the face of the trauma. No matter what happened to us, we have the freedom to realize our wholeness and live by it. It is our birthright, and no trauma and no hardship or loss can take that from us. We always have the opportunity to be happy and to find a way to love ourselves. At any point of our life, we are free to let that love be stronger than whatever experiences we have or have had. That intention, that love, is the path back to an awareness of our own innocence and joy and ability to be open, accepting, generous, joyful and playful. And along that path comes a sense of spaciousness and freedom. Not as a difficult, dragged-out, deep-seated, effortful reorientation to something better, before trauma stuck. But as a natural consequence of connecting with our true inner light, a light that shines so much brighter than anything that has ever happened to us; something as obvious as the sun rising every morning no matter what happened the night before.

> Justifications, clarifications, explanations, rational-
> izations . . .
> Debunking, rearranging, declaring, proclaiming . . .
> Like little evasive politicians, red in their faces,
> cursing and cooing.
> I listened into the quiet and dropped them all
> Then I panicked and ran right back into my
> mind, looking everywhere for them,
> as if I had just lost my closest, most endearing friends

And quickly I found them all again, as well as
their cousins and acquaintances
But what am I doing with them all that I haven't
done a million times before?
Do I really want to find them?
Or do I finally veer off onto the path without a map
Where my name can be forgotten
Where my form, my shape, my voice, all that I
know as myself, melts into the ocean
Can I find the courage?
Can I let it float away, dissipate into spaces and
places that I don't control?
Can I let myself live?
Nameless, formless, aimless
Can I trust what I say I believe?
Can I take a small, tentative step on that transpar-
ent, cold, thin ice?
Can I be that open?
Can I let myself be?
Can I walk through the tunnel of so much noise
and adrenaline?
Trusting that I will find what I came here for
That I will be able to breathe with the lungs of cosmos
My heart beating with the universal heart
To take that step through the tunnel of so much noise
Not only to survive
But to thrive

Without the conclusion
Without the resolution
In that aimless place
The untouched space
The ultimate revolution

If we are lost on paths of anger and revenge, tapping into our own light, our source, allowing ourselves to get quiet enough to hear what is *really* true, really powerful, really real, will set us free. We would not be doing this to save anyone else. We would be doing it because we are committed to our own well-being and want to find our way out of our own traumatic internal echoes. We are doing it because we have decided to live beyond the thoughts that let adrenaline push us into ditches. We are wholeheartedly committed to live beyond the circular cognitive ruminations that never open any doors, don't solve any problems, and don't allow us to see the sun, the moon, or the stars in their true glory. And so it shall be. Not through effort and pain but through becoming truly receptive, going beyond the noise.

Mary Oliver's poem "The Journey" is a beautiful description of the not-always-easy process of leaving those deeply ingrained thought processes and habits behind, trying to find the path through that noise, standing one's ground through "the voices" that "kept shouting their bad advice," through "a wild night," a "road full of fallen branches and stones," and in spite of the wind that "pried with its stiff fingers." Oliver's poem depicts someone who has made up their mind about where they are going and what they want. "The Journey" is about someone who, little by little, notices the noise, the voices of those bad advisers, begin to subside and move into the background. "The stars began to burn through the sheets of clouds" and a "new voice," which the protagonist "slowly recognized as [their] own," moved [them] more deeply into the world, as they were "determined to do the only thing [they] could do—determined to save the only life [they] could save."

The way we save our own lives, or rather, the way we come to realize that we are and always were saved, is by letting our internalized voices of hate and regret and self-punishment stay behind. We don't have to chase them off, but we can make choices about what we want to focus on most of the time. When we let this happen, forgiveness (as in the absence of resentment) is the natural consequence.

> "To forgive is to set a prisoner free and discover
> that the prisoner was you."
> —Louis B. Smedes

We are both the prisoner and the savior.

And as we find our way beyond our stories, we are free to love again. And love finds us. Our love expresses something that is whole. No one else is asked to perform the impossible task of healing what is broken in us. No one else is responsible for our happiness. No one on the outside, ultimately, has the power to make us miserable or happy. Our power is on the inside. That's what we keep tuning in to. And we get better and better at simply staying connected with our inner source. Our love, free from regret and bondage, becomes a sacred act.

> *If you are in the track of love, you have no*
> *obligations, no expectations. You don't feel sorry for*
> *yourself or for your partner. . . . In the track of love,*
> *there is no if; there are no conditions. I love you for*
> *no reason, with no justification. I love you the way*
> *you are, and you are free to be the way you are.*
> —Don Miguel Ruiz, *Mastery of Love*

This becomes possible when we understand who we are. Our place in the whole. Our connectedness with everything. The freedom we all have to be on this planet in that joyful, playful, creative mode that we so often fail to cash in on.

But by the time we do realize the creative possibilities and the freedom we have as human beings on this beautiful earth, we have understood that the work is not in fixing something or someone on the outside. We also know that it's okay to stay with something or someone and it's okay to leave too. Life doesn't judge us. Our inner being loves us no matter what we do. There is no right or wrong. There is however, being tuned into and in harmony with our inner being or straying away from it. As people, we constantly do and undo things in our lives. It's natural and doesn't need to be stigmatized. We create beginnings and endings. We make rules and we find opportunities to break them. We build things and we destroy them. In my work as a therapist, there is a format. There are ways that therapists and clients are with each other. And that does help the process. It's not some total free-for-all. But when a therapist has the guts to sometimes—when intuition tells her or him to say something unexpected about themselves or give a client an extra couple of minutes to finish their thought or give a hug in spite of the expectation that gratifying a client is to be avoided at all costs (who came up with this one?!)—the client responds, and the process actually becomes more vital and productive.

Recently, a female client stood up to me, complained about the treatment, and declared that she had found a new therapist. As we worked this through, I realized that her making this stand was her greatest achievement during our work together. When the end of our last session came I gave her my full blessing and a big hug. My client loved the hug, and she loved the idea that I had broken the rule for her. And she loved that I had fully accepted that she was done with me being her therapist and supported her in leaving me rather than trying to prevent her from doing what she felt was right for her.

When we break the rules, when we follow our heart rather than some external expectations, when we reach out to someone with our hearts full of acceptance, because the energy, the love, is there at that moment and we don't worry about it being right or wrong or long-lasting or socially acceptable, it *is* right. It's the right thing because it means we have an open heart, and our wish to love someone is stronger than our fear, stronger than our judgments, stronger than anything anyone can say to us or about us. When we are guided by love and caring about another person as well as about ourselves unconditionally, we cannot go wrong.

> *Your task is not to seek for love, but merely to seek*
> *and find all the barriers within yourself that you*
> *have built against it.*
> —RUMI, THE ESSENTIAL RUMI

To love someone else requires self-love. To be able to love ourselves, we have to know who we are and who we are not. We have to come home to our true heart, our source, and know that all else is impermanent, ultimately insignificant, and not something we need to obsess about. When we come home to ourselves, when we can sit in a place of awareness, watching our physical lives unfolding like a dream before us, we are free to see and both enjoy the ebb and the flow of things. From here, we can truly love someone else and let them love us too. And because we are willing to lose our neurotic investment in all that isn't really us, our expression of love becomes powerful.

Edna St. Vincent Millay, in her "Renascence" poem, illustrates the power of this love, as she describes how "the soul can split the sky in two, and let the face of love shine through."

There is no limit to what love can do when we tune into our own heart and live our lives guided by our heart rather than our minds, feelings, sensations, and experiences. When our heart guides us, we can process very difficult experiences in less time and more effectively. Our heart metabolizes so much better than our minds, have you noticed? There is no limit to what an open heart can handle. But very often, because we have not yet figured out how to live openheartedly, how to welcome and love our life the way it is, our relationships are less about acceptance and respect and more about regret, jealousy, possessiveness, and fear. We falsely develop the belief that people and experiences can hurt us, and we need to shut down and buckle up in the face of challenge. Nothing could be further from the truth. The experiences are there as opportunities for us to become more open, more aware of what we want in our lives, softer and more perceptive rather than tougher, harder, and more closeminded.

Whenever we are motivated primarily by our fears, whether we are afraid of having or losing or connecting or experiencing new things or old things, love cannot be at the forefront. When there is a lot of fear there is simply less space for expressions of love.

The Toltec spiritualist Don Miguel Ruiz writes in *The Mastery of Love,*:

> *"Love is always kind. Fear is always unkind. With fear we are full of obligations, full of expectations, with no respect, avoiding responsibility, and feeling sorry for ourselves... We feel victimized by everything, we feel angry or sad or jealous or betrayed."*

When we love and welcome ourselves, our lives, and each other without regret and with full and wholehearted acceptance, we are free. And we have clarity. It is obvious to us what we should do. Stay with someone, leave, do something for someone or not do it, work hard or rest. Nothing is in the way of us listening to our instinct. Sometimes, when we are not welcoming ourselves the way we are, when we don't listen, when we refuse to be receptive to ourselves, our self-rejection shows up in our bodies.

Why do we stop caring about ourselves when we need it the most? Of course, the reasons for denying ourselves any form of self care vary in as many ways as there are people and ways of thinking and feeling. But I do think that very often, when someone lets themselves fall apart physically, it can be a form of self-protection, a kind of boundary put up as a buffer between a person and their outside world.

One example of lack of self care is not eating enough or eating too much. When it comes to being overweight, it is of course not always rooted in psychological issues. A love of food, not enough movement, metabolic issues, medical conditions, preferences etc. are sometimes the reason for being heavy. However, commonly, putting on extra pounds can be a form of protection against what a person perceives as other people's judgment. It may have originated from the outside. It may have to do with an early and ongoing critical environment that eventually was internalized; the lack of appreciation and acceptance becoming part of that person's own thought patterns.

Forty-year-old Karl, an accomplished professional, started therapy because he wanted to learn how to take care of himself more consistently and effectively. He was very heavy, had a hard time motivating himself to take regular showers, and had a lot of self-percecutory thoughts that often were so intensively anxiety ridden that he projected them outward, often feeling that other people had let him down or taken advantage of him or not recognized him sufficiently. Karl was an only child. His father, let's call him Hendrick, was successful in his own right, though with very low self-esteem. Hendrick identified with Karl and criticized him constantly. Karl, in turn, identified with his father and, without knowing it, accepted the criticism as his own. So now, not only did Karl have a father who kept sending him critical, devaluing messages, but also, and much, much worse, he had himself and his own self-judgment and self-hatred to contend with. And eventually, his physical state began to respond to his unresolved inner conflicts in a very tangible and powerful way.

Recently, Karl told me that he had re-entered therapy for a little while but that he quit going a few months into it because he felt that the therapist was openly and overwhelmingly judgmental. That may be so. Heaven only knows, many therapists would be better off in a different line of work. We are so often compelled to work with others because it seems like a shortcut to our own mental health. We are so used to living in the middle of inter-relational crisis that we recreate it in our workplace. In many cases the better choice would be for us therapists to change careers or at least take some time off to find a way to become a little more harmonious with ourselves before we attempt to relate to someone else's issues. I trust that Karl did what was best for him. But if he ever ventures into therapy again, it's not unlikely that the theme of the relationship with the therapist will have something to do with judgments. He may again experience the therapist as overly critical.

We do tend to bring up in very real and convincing ways the things we need help with. Karl needs help with self-judgment. If he learns how not to judge himself so harshly, he will return to self-care. Self-judgment and lack of self-acceptance almost inevitably show up in our physical appearance. We keep looking to create external expressions for our internal experience. The most immediate reflection of that internal experience is indeed our bodies. We may be looking to validate our internal experience of being wrong, of not being good enough, not attractive, and not available for closeness by keeping the extra pounds. The extra weight is holding the other at a safe distance. Literally. The problem with this strategy is obvious. The weight does not only fail to protect us from judgment, it evokes it. Self-punishment in any form never cured anyone. Buddha found that out the hard way, spending months and months depriving himself of the essentials in his quest for enlightenment. Deprivation and excessive gratification are not that dissimilar. The judgment in the case of excess weight does not usually originate in some outside body snob condemning us for being fat, lazy, and out of shape. Most of the time it's our own thought processes that brought us there, and no one on the outside can change that. Ultimately, there is nothing anyone else can do about where we are on any level.

Even when we do experience other people's criticisms, we have a choice. We can either elaborate on how other people judge us, why they do it, what it means to us, what it means about them, how to make it stop and so on. We could surround ourselves with judgmental people to reinforce this idea that is so familiar to us. It would be like throwing dry logs into an already existing fire. But if we want that fire to subside, if we got tired of living in that world of adrenaline and dejection, rage and loneliness, we could stop throwing more firewood onto this kind of situation. We might trace the origin of those very uncomfortable flames, the real source of the negative judgment, and we would find it in our very own thought patterns. Looking honestly at ourselves, we have all the tools we need to transform that judgment into acceptance. And when we see clearly what we are actually doing to ourselves—hurting ourselves with negative thoughts, punishing ourselves by putting low-quality food into our bodies, eating too much or too little without enjoyment and care, pushing our bodies beyond the breaking point, forcing it to do things it's not prepared to do or weakening our physical system by not providing enough challenge—our harsh self-treatment becomes a little less automatic. Our bodies are sacred. As the former Ethiopian emperor Haile Selassie, in his Rastafari speech on religion and spirituality, said: "The temple of the most high begins with the human body, which houses our life, essence of our existence."

It *holds* "the most high," but it *is* not the most high. I think this is an important distinction that puts a lot of concerns related to our bodies into perspective. While understanding the beauty and sacred nature of our bodies and of all physical manifestations of life, we can tune into what is beyond it. We can remind ourselves that, ultimately, there is really nothing to work out. Nothing to sort through or repair. We would know that all that stuff we do is not at all fundamental in the context of who we really are. And that from this broader perspective, ultimately, what we do with your physical selves isn't the most important. Our bodies are temporary, impermanent, and will return to dust. The thing we really need to know in order to restore harmony is not just related to restoring our bodies. And it's also not about figuring out, straightening out, catching, disciplining, punishing, or rewarding our thoughts. All that is background stuff. Through meditation and stillness, we could reconnect with our real selves and with real clarity. We could tune in with the one that watches everything come and go. The nonreactive, non-defensive part of ourselves. We could decide that we want to spend most of our time here tuning in to the truth about who we are, knowing that we are so much greater and infinitely more vast and free than our ideas, conceptualizations, judgments, thought processes, feelings, bodies, hang-ups, etc.

Words,
Cheered on by restless minds
Little cunning games
Throughout time
Somersaulting, cartwheeling, crawling, and climbing
Oohing and awing
Looping and leaping
Begging and pleading
Defending pretending condescending recommending
Like dust in the wind they rise and they fall
Oblivious to it all
When every single word has been used up
Truth is still standing
Unimpressed, Unafraid
Untattered, Uncorrupted
Open and Beautiful
Like a field full of Flowers
Like all the shapes of the Moon
Like the Sun melting into the Ocean

Angelina was a fellow student and a good friend of mine from when I was studying psychoanalysis at the

Postgraduate Center for Mental Health in New York City. She was a substantial Jamaican woman, a free spirit, radiant like the sun. I loved her nonrestricted, unconventional take on life, people, and their processes. During the time we studied together, I was becoming increasingly interested in Buddhism. I remember sitting on the sidewalk outside our institute one day reading a quote about the various processes of the body decaying and turning into dust. It was a kind of meditation focused on watching one's body turn into the earth, of letting it go and smiling through it all in awareness of the blessings of impermanence. I read it to Angelina who came by on her way back into the building for another one of our classes. She was enthralled by it. From then on, every time I saw her, she asked me to reread it to her. Why she wouldn't read it herself, I don't know. The quote ended with "I smile." Angelina laughed every time I got to that part, enjoying it as the ultimate punchline. One weekend, she came with me and my husband to the beach. She sat on the sand facing the water in her black bathing suit with a little cute skirt at the bottom. She was so beautiful as she sat there smiling into the water.

"I love to be close to the ocean. It heals me," she said and smiled her incredibly open and warm smile. We went to a restaurant near the beach and Angelina, who was invariably broke, ordered more or less everything on the menu. My husband and I looked at her with big eyes. She enjoyed every bite as fully as I have ever seen anyone enjoying anything. Everything seemed to be sacred to her. As we drove Angelina to the train station that night, she was beaming. She said she had the time of her life and was so happy. Then one day, Angelina disappeared from the program. I kept calling her, asking everyone where she was, but no one knew, and she never returned my calls. It was months until I heard from her. Then suddenly her sister called and told me that Angelina was at a hospice in the Bronx, with cancer, and had just a brief time left to live. She had asked me to come visit.

She was half her size and very weak when I got there, but she still had that love and light pouring out of her somehow. She asked me to read the quote about dying again. She smiled faintly as I got to the punchline. I left the hospital and even though I was very familiar with the area, I somehow got lost, riding around in buses for hours, tears down my cheeks, before I found my way home. Angelina had died that afternoon, a couple of minutes after I left. During her forty-something years on this planet, she had understood everything there is to know about impermanence and wholehearted acceptance and enjoyment without attachment. Every time I think of her, I smile.

Many men and women are perpetually dissatisfied with their bodies. It's too big, too round, not round enough at the right places and too round at other places, too long, too short, too dark, too pale. We are overly identified with our bodies. We refuse to acknowledge it as something temporary. Something that, like our thoughts and feelings, our experiences and our physical sensations, will come and go. But also, we are not used to recognizing our bodies for all the incredible things it—in intimate, inseparable collaboration with our brains—can do. Instead we overinvest in, overvalue, and criticize our own bodies and other people's bodies for how they appear. All the while our hearts keep on beating, our lungs breathing, our blood pumping, our nerves and muscles and bones continuing to receive signals from our brains, helping us move, feel, sense, and accomplish the most astonishing miracles every moment of our lives. The way I see it, we have very little reason to punish and criticize our bodies. If we spent a little more time thinking about what it can do and less time obsessing about its appearance, we would be naturally inclined to care for it, for ourselves, in ways that would most definitely improve our physical health if not revolutionize, not just our physical health, but our appearance as well!

Another obstacle to our physical well-being, contentment, and wellness has to do with listening. We override ourselves. We are so caught up in our mind, our thoughts, that we have a hard time *feeling* ourselves.

When we listen, really listen, we naturally do the right thing. We develop our receptive ability. When we act as if our thoughts are more important than any other aspect of ourselves, when we are identified with our stories of what happened to us in the past, who we are, who we are not, what and when we eat and drink and when we're not, when and how we move—all that noise keeps us from feeling ourselves as we are now. If we were to really listen to our own systems in an openhearted, nonjudgmental way—our heartbeat, our breathing, the way we move, what we feel and sense—we would be very likely to fall in love. If we could be like babies again, looking at our own hand movements, fascinated, slowly realizing, once again, that those hands can move, reach for someone's hair, grab a toy or a hand, we would very quickly stop complaining about all the things our bodies cannot do. And we would spontaneously want to do everything we can to take good care of ourselves. And with that kind of appreciation, our bodies would grow stronger and even more beautiful. Our bodies would be responding to our thoughts and feelings of gratitude and awe. We would fully understand the deep appreciation that poet Yusef Komunyakaa expresses in "Anodyne," as he describes how he "loves this body, made to weather the storm ... the liver's ten kinds of desire and the kidney's lust for sugar ... this solo and ragtime jubilee behind the left nipple, because I know I was made to wear out at least one hundred angels."

If we could relate to ourselves in this way, with deep appreciation if we were to see the underlying beauty in everything alive, including ourselves and each other, we would stop being so exacting. We wouldn't have to put a bunch of conditions on ourselves and others in order to enjoy each other's company. While we are very slow to learn this, no relationship has ever succeeded without at least some measure of unconditional love. It's the only absolutely necessary ingredient to any loving connection. The idea being that we are not responsible for each other's happiness. Without this unconditional love, for as long as we are humans, our relationships with ourselves, as well as with each other, will involve a lot of suffering. The same goes for the way we relate to life in general. When we approach life in a conditional manner, happiness and peace feel very far away.

We will experience challenges. Our loved ones will die. Companies will downsize. Whether we did something or didn't do it, we will look bad from time to time. Our reputation will undergo ups and downs. The sun will go up and down. We'll sleep well and we'll sleep poorly. We'll be close and far away from the ones we love, literally and figuratively. We'll have physical pain and we'll be free of physical pain. When we relate conditionally to our life and each other, we are like leaves blowing in the wind, one day sad and upset, the next day happy and satisfied, all dependent on what is happening in our lives. I think it's possible to be alive on this planet and find an independence, a kind of deep trust and love of life, where it doesn't matter if a tree falls on our house or doesn't. With this independent approach to life, we can see the love and the power pulsing through everything. True freedom is welcoming life as it is. And interestingly enough, when we find this kind of freedom, we also find that things in our life start to work out with much more ease.

I will return to this idea of inner knowing, of influencing our lives and being an active participant in the way things turn out in chapter 5. For now, I'd like to focus on the idea of loving what is because it's such an important part of being happy that if we have that, the way our lives turn out, the details of it, simply becomes less important.

Living in an openhearted way allows our lives to become more rhythmic, more expansive, more adventurous, and miraculous. We don't shut down in the face of the disasters in our life, we allow them to make us even more openhearted. We learn that there is a sacred rhythm to everything, and when we find that rhythm everything is truly like a river—there is grace in our movement and in our life, there is an unconditionality that makes absolutely everything beautiful. It's not really what happens to us that make things heavy and stuck. It's that we consider it a thing to regret, a thing that's wrong or insufficient or permanent, something to do away with and fix, something we need to become desperate and fearful and panicky about. The alternative to this kind of rigorous policing and categorizing and condemning of our own life events is so much more fun:

> Dance, when you're broken open.
> Dance, if you've torn the bandage off.
> Dance in the middle of fighting.
> Dance in your blood.
> Dance, when you're perfectly free.
>
> —RUMI, "DANCE IN YOUR BLOOD,"
> TRANSLATED BY COLEMAN BARKS

4

Letting Go—Flowing

You are not a drop in the ocean; you are the entire ocean in a drop.

—RUMI

It cannot be found because it's not lost
Not seen with eyes restlessly scanning the horizon
Not reached by searching, hoping, losing hope
We searched anyway, our hearts sinking
Days, months, years, lifetimes

It became a prison
We tried to forget what we wanted to find
We don't need what we want, we said
Or want what we need
It didn't make it true
We were so slow to realize
We went to all the wrong allies
The answer was too simple for our complicated minds
Blinded by our search
We found nothing
We gave up and found silence
We sat down by the road and looked up at the
rising sun
Some birds were chirping and the tall grass
swayed in the gentle wind
A strange joy exploded in our bellies
We had been there all along

Letting go of important matters in our lives often feels like a counterintuitive process. We hold on for dear life to things way after their expiration date and long after we even remember why it was so crucial to us that we didn't lose them. It all becomes tight and contracted, fearful and rigid, pretty quickly. But whenever we realize that we are part of everything and that everything, including the things that fall out of our lives, is sacred, the very idea of losing becomes less intense. If we really felt that kind of connection and unity with everything alive, we could look at the hawk circling above our heads and know that in some sense, we are not as tied down by gravity as we tend to think. We too have wings, and that hawk is intimately connected with us and our lives.

If we lived in the awareness of this unity, we would look at the one person that annoys us most and know they are us. We would look at the flowers, the sun, the most beautiful horse we have ever seen, or the glitter in the vast ocean, or the deep yellow and orange and red of the leaves in October, and know how limitless we are, how beautiful and free and wealthy we are. With this awareness, we would never truly have to let go of anything, because we would know that whatever we are losing will just keep coming back to us in a different form. We talk a lot about letting go, but most of us have trouble understanding what it is; that winning and losing really is the same thing.

While we may know this concept in theory, in our everyday lives most of us have yet to learn how to really live it. The smallest detail that doesn't go our way throws us off. We want what we want and we don't have much experience with losing and being okay with it. We don't know how to trust the ebb and flow of things. So we keep up the good fight. We regret what is, we hold on to things with our whitening knuckles as if our lives depended on it. The problem is, when we are attached to something in a possessive, obsessive way, our energy is blocked and nothing goes well. It's only when we are willing to lose something, that we actually find it. When we are connected to our source, our own inner source that taps into all light, all love, all life, all around us, we understand how truly wealthy we are on every level, how we need nothing and can have *everything*. My daughter Lina, via a letter board, captured this idea in a poem called "My Adventure Longing for Spring":

I am so universally tired
I am nothing original
I am the soaring hawks
I am life in the roaring rivers
I love you waters rinsing through me in the winter
You make everything old and new

Lina is an unconventional thinker who has no trouble with the idea of everything's interconnectedness. She gets that it's not her individuality that protects her, but rather her willingness to see beyond it and find the whole. I think the fact that she understands this helps her stay happy in the middle of the autism tornadoes that her life is filled with. I also think this is what will slowly, gradually help her leave autism challenges behind.

For many people however, particularly in Western cultures, life can often feel counterintuitive. We believe somehow that holding on, being on guard, hunkering down with our ideas and defense systems and our individuality is what protects us. When I first got to New York City, I lived in Queens with a couple of other people. They were all photographers. I was aspiring to write freelance articles for Swedish newspapers and magazines. One of my roommates was a guy who, right after I arrived there, got mugged three times in a row. Why? It happened once. He got scared, tried to protect himself and, consequently, was robbed two more times in less than one week. It kept happening until he found a way to let the experience go and stop making his life about whether or not he was going to get robbed. We all have our own individual version of this. We focus so much on trying to avoid what we are afraid of and we are so loyal to our fears and preoccupied by them that we tend to re-create it. So it is with the person leaving an abusive relationship but still focusing on the abuser to such an extent that their next relationship is very likely to become abusive yet again. Only when we let go, it lets go of us.

How is it that we are more protected when we go against our learned instincts and stop trying to defend ourselves? Why are we safer when we no longer try to shield ourselves from the storms of human experience? Why are we happier when we stop searching frenetically for what we think will make us happy? Why are we fuller and more satisfied when we let ourselves be empty?

It's so counterintuitive. We are still, undeniably, gatherers and hunters, and yet, the more we do what we think we need to do to keep sane, to keep everything running smoothly, or at all, the more miserable we get. We have a million and one ideas of how to fix things, and yet, nothing gets fixed until we are not just begrudgingly okay with what's happening in our lives but at peace with it and with ourselves.

No thought pattern, no encouraging words, no defensive justification, no effort of mind, no possession, no relationship, no position or reputation, ever brought anyone happiness. We want to be happy. And I am not at all saying that there is anything wrong with what we want. Quite the contrary! But most of the time, our fears, our trepidation, our stubborn staring at the stuff we don't like about our lives and our situation take us straight to hell. The answer is so simple. Letting our breathing become a little softer and slower. Opening our eyes and trusting the whole. Letting something from the inside hold us.

> Something opens our wings. Something
> makes boredom and hurt disappear.
> Someone fills the cup in front of us.
> We taste only sacredness.
>
> —RUMI, "DANCE IN YOUR BLOOD,"
> TRANSLATED BY COLEMAN BARKS

It's only when we realize that everything is sacred—
and that we are one with the whole world and can fly,
swim, run, crawl, have everything, have nothing, win
and lose, be in the middle of darkness and light, laugh
and cry, love and hate, be blind and see—that we find
who we truly are. What we experience as separation,
what we are accustomed to think of as polar opposites,
inconsolable differences, are all one. The contradictions
create the whole. So there is no reason to hold on to
anything. The paradox doesn't separate, it unites, it creates life, it brings us home. When we fully embrace
everything, we come face-to-face with grace, God,
source, Allah, Buddha, Krishna, Christ—whatever you
want to call it or not call it. The non-separated space.
Oneness. Truth.

In 2009, at my mother's funeral, my youngest daughter Elsa and I were sitting in the front pew in an old
church watching the people who had been close to my
mother walking up to the coffin to say goodbye. Lina,
who had regressed into autism a few years prior, was a
little too active for this event and had to stay outside,
walking, running, and playing with our babysitter Valerie,
who had come with us to Sweden to make this trip more
doable. As Elsa and I were sitting there in that beautiful
old, white stone church, Elsa looked at everyone's sad
faces with big, surprised eyes. She turned to me and with
her sweet, loud, three-year-old voice she concluded:

"Mama, why is everyone so sad? Grandma isn't really dead!"

From her innocent child perspective, she knew that her grandmother was going home, to a place of no resistance. She knew that everything was fine and there was no reason to regret anything. She understood that life and death are not in opposition and that winning and losing was the same thing. Why try to hold on to someone who was ready to go home? Why regret something so natural and predictable as dying? Of course there is a sadness about not having a loved one around as a physical presence. But to resist someone's death is not dissimilar from regretting that after summer comes fall, then winter, then spring, then summer yet again.

Death is the foundation for life. One is part of the other. Death, in a way, is no different from birth. It is different angles of the same thing. Death saves us when we are beyond saving. It's a little bit like what Michael A. Singer writes about in *The Untethered Soul*:

> *When the drop of consciousness that knows itself as an individual drifts back far enough, it becomes like the drop that falls into the ocean. The Atman (Soul) falls into the Paramatman (Supreme Soul). The individual consciousness falls into the Universal Oneness. And that's it.*

Singer describes what can happen when we meditate. But he could easily be talking about passing from life to death.

There is something about agenda, individuality, ego, control, fear, suspiciousness, needing to have things proven to us, needing something on the outside to compensate us for our lack of faith, that gets in the way of us living our lives fully. If we truly want to find, we have to be willing to lose. Not in a regretful, bitter way but in a joyful, confident, free, trusting and open way. We kind of need to die before we can truly find our life. We need to allow laughter to bubble up inside us before our manifested life can support that joy. We need to see our own part in the whole. We need to dare to jump, see in the dark, know before knowing. Mother Earth is willing to do it before every new season. There is no other way for new leaves to grow than the old ones drying up and falling off, branches left naked until spring. In this way, death is not really death in the way we usually look at it. Death is life. The end is the beginning. Or, as Kahlil Gibran, in "The Prophet" (1923), wrote:

> You would know the secret of death.
> But how shall you find it unless you seek it in the heath of life?
> The owl whose night bound eyes are blind unto the day cannot unveil the mystery of light.

For life and death are one, even as the river and
the sea are one.

Good things come from understanding that death isn't
something we have to desperately avoid and life isn't
something we have to frenetically cling to. We are part
of everything and everything is part of us. If we are
everything what do we have to fear? What are we lacking? Regretting? If we are both the problem and the
solution, why worry? If darkness and light illuminate
each other, why prefer one to the other? We are much
more beautiful, large, limitless, connected, and whole
than we think. We are much more incredible, vast, sacred,
and miraculous than we can possibly describe in words!

This awareness that lays dormant in so many of us is a
revelation anyone can wake up to. When people talk
about enlightenment and spiritual awakening, it often
sounds like they are describing something unattainable.
Something that is so far away from them that it would
take years and decades of hard work, dreary self-sacrifice
and dull repetition and restriction. The good news is that
they too already have everything. They don't have to go
anywhere to find it. We don't have to find the path of
sacrifice and suffering to find home. We don't have to
find the path at all. We are already home.

Eva Dahlgren, a Swedish singer, wrote a song called
"Jag År Gud" (I am God, 1991) that illuminates the joy

of being one with everything. In this song about the power of knowing who we really are, Dahlgren describes how every little gray stone "carries an eternity" and every little flower possesses a dignity that is godly. This beautiful and inspired song is also about how we, as humans, get disoriented in the moment we forget this interconnectedness. The remedy, as Dahlgren sees it, lies in heart, in the idea of feeling "the width of [one's] heart, where the whole world exists," were "every soul is a God."

If it is really true that we are energetically and intrinsically part of the whole world, whether we are moving backward or forward doesn't matter.

One of my clients was a successful painter in her seventies. She was actively pursuing her art, enjoying every aspect of her work except when her work was exhibited. Every time one of her shows opened, she dreaded waiting for feedback, the possibility of other people buying or not buying her art, the feeling of being exposed to the judgment of the world. Working with this woman for a few years, I recognized the pattern. We were sitting in my living room talking about the fact that she had some version of this anxiety right after the opening of every show she'd ever had. And there had been quite a few! I glanced at the swing hanging from the doorway, so often used during that time by Lina to provide her with sufficient sensory input. I walked up to it and pushed the swing back and then let go of it. Predictably, it swung forward. Then back. Then forward.

"Do you see this?" I said to my client. "You see how the backward motion is a prerequisite for going forward? And look what happens if I try to stifle the backward motion and try to force to swing to move only upward! There is no flow, no movement, no energy."

The rest of the session we talked about how, when we resist the natural ebb and flow of our lives, we stifle our own movement. Regretting our losses makes us less available, open, and prepared for the things we want. No one tries to run out to the horizon at sunset and stop the sun from setting. No one tries to prevent the moon from circling Earth. It waxes and wanes regardless of what we do. Similarly, it's futile to try to stop our lives from its natural progress. Resisting the experiences we are having. Shutting down in the face of things that we consider unfortunate and undesirable. It would be more effective to figure out a way to welcome what has already happened, find something about it that we can connect with in an openhearted way and see the value and the beauty in it. Live happily regardless of the temporary situation regarding something we want. Not as some kind of strained and fake Pollyanna approach but honestly, wholeheartedly, and decisively, simply because it's more fun and more pleasant to welcome the ups and downs of our lives rather than regretting and rejecting them.

I once wrote one third of a book only to see the document vanish right in front of my eyes. Left were only some distorted letters on one page. On a different day I would have panicked about losing all the stuff that I had written. This time, however, I felt okay with it, and instead of regretting the lost document and having to start all over again, I felt excitement about now having the option of writing something completely different. I was being blessed with a blank page. Because one thing was clear to me: if I didn't find a way to retrieve this document easily, I would not go back and try to rewrite it. It happened. And I decided to approach it in the way of least resistance. And at this particular time I had enough perspective to be at peace with that. And then, of course, my energy shifted and my document magically reappeared.

I recently had a phone conversation with one of my closest friends about letting go of things in our lives that aren't working. We talked about the relief in recognizing that it's not conducive to one's happiness to keep on fighting for something that clearly isn't yielding. After picking up Lina at school, as we were driving across the Hudson River, I felt that kind of spaciousness that always comes with free thought. I had the awesome realization that nothing really matters all that much and everything is fine just the way it is. I saw a large bird sitting on one of the lampposts along the bridge and said to Lina, "I wonder what kind of bird that is?" As we came closer, it turned out to be a bald eagle. I have never seen an eagle on that bridge or anywhere in that busy, densely populated area, but frequently when I am where I am supposed to be, on higher ground, in complete and unconditional harmony with myself and life, unattached to outcome, I see an eagle.

That night, I had a dream of being in an airport, trying to make it to the gate. Over the years I have made many futile dream attempts to get on the right planes at the right time. Only this one ended differently from all my other airport dreams.

In this dream my father, and intermittently my ex-husband, were there too. We were traveling together. Just as it was time to get to our flight's gate, I realized that my plane ticket looked more like a movie ticket. Then I noticed that I didn't have my bags with me. I saw my father and my ex disappearing in the crowd of travelers and wondered if I would be able to find my way even if I did manage to locate my bags. I found them in the waiting area, where we had been sitting, but they were empty. A tall, broad man in uniform was standing nearby. I asked him if he thought my ticket would be valid and if he could show me the way to the gate. He agreed, though it became clear that he was quite distracted and also not very optimistic about me being able to make it on time.

Eventually the uniformed agent turned into a woman in a red flouncy skirt. The woman, who struck me as a bit off-kilter, was engrossed in pouring some kind of watery fluid into white rubber vials on a tray, and as I reminded her that she was to take me to the gate she reluctantly packed up her gear and walked me there. As we got to the gate, the man at the desk was Jermael (someone I dated years ago). He saw me and shouted, "It doesn't matter about the ticket, you can make it, as long as you celebrate transvestites!" I yelled back "Okay, yeah, let's celebrate!" Then the woman in the red skirt brought me to a dirt field. At the edge of it was a tremendous heap of rusty metal. I saw that we needed to get to a field below, which would involve jumping down the steep metal mountain. I suddenly felt much bolder and told the woman, "Don't worry, my friend, I'm going to show you how to jump, and then you'll be able to follow!" I ran across the field and jumped down, onto the metal mountain, making lots of noise when the metal pile yielded under my weight. The woman jumped after me, boldly too, drawn into the adventure of it all. She too made a lot of noise as she bumped down the pile. At this point, the idea of catching the plane seemed secondary. It was about the thrill of jumping, getting to exciting and new places.

I think of dreams as a way of processing experiences in our lives. When interpreting dreams, mine or others, I always ask myself, what is the dreamer trying to accomplish in the dream. Less restricted by awake consciousness, taboos, convention, time and expectations, our dreams are extremely creative ways to understand ourselves and our lives better. It is not just processing and overcoming difficult experiences but it's also discovering and creating new awareness, new possibility and direction.

In my dream, I decided to find a new way of living my life. My childhood, my marriage, my baggage, the validity of my ticket, all of it eventually ceased to be important. In the process of trying to do what I have done so many times before, I realized there was a different path, less linear, much more fun and adventurous. I found freedom and boldness, and a sense that I could do things my own way. The heap of metal might have something to do with the big pile of rusty metal that I have collected out on the field in front of my house and put by the gate. Every time I passed it, I was reminded of all the tasks I need to do that I haven't yet done on the farm.

But in this dream I turned that metal into a mountain that I could jump into and land in a different kind of field, with a sense of relief and lightness. The huge pile of metal yielded to my enthusiasm and joy and reminds me of the enormous sandpits of my childhood that my brothers and I used to jump into when we were young. It was an incredible sense of freedom to leap into that soft, damp sand, gliding, rolling, tumbling all the way to the bottom. It was a feeling of almost flying that made everything seems so possible and expansive.

A pivotal aspect of any kind of liberation is that when we are willing to lose, when we let ourselves give up our struggle and be here now, and love what is right in front of us, we are more available for everything that we want. Whether that is getting something back that we lost or doing something new or different. Most of us are very slow learners in this area. On the last day of the school year of Elsa's elementary school, I picked her up along with her two BFFs to bring them back to our apartment. I leaned my bike against a green parking signpost outside their school building and, in the commotion of my little group of after-schoolers, I walked home with them, forgetting all about the bike. Six hours later, after the friends were dropped off at their apartments, I suddenly remembered the bike. I sprinted down the street, and, to my great amazement, it was still there leaning against that green metal pole, unlocked, right where I had left it.

I'd had two mountain bikes in the city before this one. The first was stolen minutes after I announced that I didn't want to own anything and wouldn't care if I lost any of my possessions—*except my bike.* The second bike, I lost right after making a similar statement—"I'm not a materialist," I proclaimed proudly, "except when it comes to my bike." The third time, with my current ride, I decided that I had finally learned my lessons and stayed away from any further bike attachments. I think that may very well be why it still stood there, untouched for six hours, on a Friday evening, in the middle of a busy New York city street.

> *You are like the space in which everything appears*
> *and disappears.*
>
> —Mooji

I think the idea is to let our experiences come and go without getting so overinvested in outcomes. To let ourselves come and go too; win and lose, laugh and cry, remember and forget, be in darkness and be in light, breathe hard and breathe softly without constantly regretting or trying to alter or undo the things that have already happened. When we understand what's real and what isn't, we automatically stop grasping for all the things, and people, that we somehow expect will alter whatever state we are trying to escape from. Our willingness to give up the constant struggle, to lose and fall in a soft, open, trusting way, and to let our illusions go, brings us closer to ourselves and a much more fulfilling, balanced, and joyful life.

I once had a client whose mother committed suicide when she was a teenager. Anna was a tall, gorgeous young woman, her big curls almost like a halo around her striking face, glittery blue eyes, and high cheekbones. No matter how casually she dressed, Anna looked like she'd just stepped off the runway. Anna was struck by grief and guilt about her mother's suicide. She came to see me in her early twenties because she had a hard time feeling her own feelings, struggling to come out of the state of numbness that her system had utilized to protect her from the powerful trauma that she had experienced. The circumstances around her mother's suicide were brutal and difficult to process. But somehow, after long periods of numbness and paralyzing guilt, this amazing young woman was eventually able to open herself even more than most people to everything that life offered to her. Through watching her mother take her own life, Anna came so close to death that she realized that life and death are not separate states. She came so far into the darkness of human emotion that she could see, on a very deep level, how darkness and light were intimately related, and each other's prerequisite.

At the beginning of our work together, Anna was very careful with what she said and how she said it. She constantly tried to clarify and specify her statements, as if afraid that her words had so much power that they could cause damage to me. She is one of the gentlest and kindest clients I have ever had, but she had learned to view herself as the destructive one. It was better that she was the one to blame for everything than to have to live in a world where the person who was responsible for her, the person who gave her life, felt that life was so painful that it had to be ended prematurely. The consequence of this defense was a sense of dullness inside. She experienced herself as boring, with nothing interesting to say to anyone. She also felt a deep need to accommodate people, protecting them from her "true" self. She was confused about what her true self was.

Gradually, Anna let herself feel the loss of her mother and see it as something that was her mother's choice, her mother's life, and very different from the life and the choices she herself would make. Little by little she began to let herself to feel joy and excitement without being overwhelmed by guilt. Her life became fuller. Anna was an artist and as she began to allow herself a life, her art flourished. Her relationship with her younger sister became more straightforward and less apologetic. She started to have higher expectations of her father. She became less accommodating to everyone around her and more present. She met a good, kind man and moved to England. She allowed herself to let go of the guilt and fear and be the vibrant, interesting and charismatic person she was here on this planet to be.

Karin Boye, in her poem "Yes of Course it Hurts" describes this fear, this ambivalence about trusting and opening and letting go that my client Anna, and most humans, struggle with. Boye uses the image of drops hanging heavy on a branch, "swelling, sliding—weight draws them down, though they go on clinging," to illustrate the uncertainty, fear and trembling ambivalence involved in wanting both to stay and fall. And how triumphant is the joy of finally letting go, forgetting the fear, plunging into the unknown, and feeling "for a second their greatest safety, rest in that trust that creates the world."

Sometimes when we lose something, there is a great sense of relief. We may not register it as such but it's there. There can be so much tense energy in holding onto something, so much effort, that it is only when we let ourselves lose it that we can finally relax.

It is in our willingness to be present and open to that interplay of contracting and expanding, holding on and letting go, opening and closing, "the two as beautifully balanced and coordinated as birds' wings," that Rumi describes in his poem "Birdwings," that we can find our freedom.

We all encounter situations that evoke a powerful desire to hold on and great fear of losing. I think it is part of the human condition and can, potentially, become part of our evolution. A couple of years after my divorce, back in New York City after living in Rhode Island for a year, I walked to the supermarket down the street from my apartment on the Upper West Side. A tall, strong-looking Colombian man working as one of the security guards at the store struck up a tentative conversation. He was a boxer. I didn't know the first thing about boxing, but the man, let's call him Luis, had something humble and sweet about him, and he was funny. I recognized that from the first moment he said hello. From then on, I had innumerable conversations with him on the street corner outside the market. Eventually we decided that I would teach him yoga and he would teach me boxing. He came to my apartment one day after his shift. My kids were over at my ex-husband's place. Luis was going to have his first yoga lesson. Not very flexible, and unused to the movement of yoga, so opposite from boxing, he spent most of the lesson resting in child's pose. I instantly connected with my new friend. He had no problem making fun of himself and his complete lack of flexibility. We both ended up on the floor, laughing hysterically. We had six months of increasing closeness, and I fell deeper in love with Luis than I had ever fallen for any man.

It was an overwhelming, uncanny kind of love. And the whole time I was with him, I felt a kind of premonition of losing him. I brought it up to him and he said there were indeed things he wanted to talk to me about, but could I give him a little more time? Six months into it, I found out that he was a recovering addict. And it wasn't because he finally opened up about it. We were standing on the street, talking and kidding around, holding hands. I told him that I was going to attend an old babysitter's wedding in Rhode Island with the kids. Luis asked if my ex-husband was going too. I confirmed that he was. Luis dropped my hand. Tony and I had reinstated our friendship after a couple of years of cold war. With Lina having severe autism, we had good reasons to try to help each other out as much as possible. For Luis, me going on a trip with my ex was threatening. I understood that, but in the world of autism, you simply have to do what works. Divorcing worked. Collaborating as a parenting team worked too. Pride and personal convenience had to give way for getting through the day. For Luis, however, our shared vacation became a trigger. He relapsed later that day. And I realized why I'd always had that fear of losing him. But by then I already loved him so much I couldn't quite let him go.

Eventually, when Luis was back in recovery, we tried again. Everything went well at first. We had big plans for the future. We were going to have a combined boxing gym and yoga studio, his and my kids running all around, playing and having fun, becoming little boxers and yogis. Somehow, things were quickly back to good and innocent. Whenever I was not with my two girls or working, I was with Luis. We had so much fun and connected so deeply. We studied Buddhism together and inspired each other in a million different ways. But somewhere deep inside, I held onto a fear of losing him. And one day I did. To another relapse, and another, and another, until I had to let go completely of the idea of a future with Luis. I no longer have any negative feelings about having had that love experience. But at the time, losing him felt like falling into a deep, black hole.

It took me a long time to understand my own involvement in this intense connection. I eventually recognized that I choose to go through that sense of powerful love and then abandonment with a sinking feeling of something dying inside to remind myself that actually, I did come out on the other side very much alive. And at this point, after this experience, I am not as afraid of losing someone I love as I was then. Like most people, I have had a lot of opportunities to practice losing what I would rather keep. I have learned to recognize that there is something that I will never lose. With that being so, a lot of other things are much easier to let go of. I have learned to allow myself the experience of relief when losing what is beginning to feel too tight and contracted. And I have gotten pretty good at knowing that what's lost always comes back in a new form and that in some sense, there is nothing that we are losing that we are not gaining at the same time. So in a roundabout way, this challenging love affair helped to make things a lot easier and a lot clearer for me.

I think it all comes down to whether or not we can remember to live in full awareness of who we are. When we do remember, we automatically become less invested in whether we are winning or losing at any given time. When we understand that there is something inside us that's perfectly whole, disappointments cease to be important. When we tune into who we are, beings of love and light, infinite and limitless, spacious and free, all the details around our physical shape, our cognitive capacities, our material possessions, our achievements, our social status, our earthly circumstances, begin to appear strangely irrelevant. If we lived in full awareness of our true identity, or maybe better put, free from individual identity, we would be able to enjoy everything and feel a deep sense of satisfaction. We wouldn't need a specific person to feel whole. Appearance wouldn't be as important to us. We would enjoy process without worrying so much about outcome. We could take steps right into the unknown and feel confident that we'll be all right. We could walk out on a negative job situation and know we would be okay. We could tell someone that we love them without being afraid of being rejected. We could learn through trial and error, without bitterness and without regret. We could let others be our teachers rather than judging them for their shortcomings. We could say what we needed to say without being afraid of losing or failing or drowning. We would be free to be ourselves in the truest sense. We would come home to ourselves and feel that this home, our true home, is safe and sacred and interesting. We could begin experiencing ourselves the way we truly are—the entire ocean in a drop.

5

Inner Knowing—Faith

Mooji TALKS ABOUT the freedom and aliveness in letting go of our superficial identity and tapping into our true, non-dual divine Being. In Mooji's teachings, suffering dissipates in the moment we recognize that we not only are part of a whole but we *are* that whole, that Supreme Being and our calling as humans is to recognize our own wholeness.

Most people, at some point in their lives, face experiences that are very difficult to process. This is the stuff that wakes us up in the middle of the night with hearts and minds racing. The terrifying, chaotic, cold, lonely places, the kind of experiences beyond the normal events in the ebb and flow of life. It feels bigger than us but we try the best we can to roll with it. Remember when you were a kid laying down on your side at the top of a hill and letting gravity roll you all the way to the bottom? Standing up after a roll like that is a dizzying experience. Similarly, in facing trauma and extraordinary hardship, we try to cope and adjust but at some point we no longer know what's up or down, north or south, backward or forward, right or wrong. We feel lost and disoriented. And it turns out, this is our chance. It is our opportunity to find something much greater than the reality we are staring at. In the face of extraordinary challenge, our mind is so discombobulated, it can no longer show us the way. We recognize that we don't have a clue of how to get to where we are going. It is at this point we may be a little more inclined to take a chance. Discard our rivers of names and forms. Tap into the deep, vast ocean inside ourselves. When we finally quiet—free of our usual rationales and justifications, no longer able to explain our own lives in our regular, slightly obsessive, neurotic ways—the most incredible thing happens. The sun shines anyway. Spring comes. Warm, soft winds. A pink evening sky. And we learn something very, very important about what it *really* holds this universe together.

Pablo Neruda, in *Fully Empowered*, "It is Born," describes the beauty that we find when we discard our identifications with names and forms and come "to the very edge where nothing at all needs saying" where "everything is absorbed through water and the sea . . . where wings open, fire is born, and everything is blue again in the morning."

How can we learn to see and know things with our heart rather than blindly following our thought processes where we put more trust in what we see than what we know? How do we develop our trust and confidence in "the pink sky" and the "blue again in the morning" independent of the current physical manifestations? How can we cultivate the kind of bravery and independence that's involved in this process? How can we foster that ability within ourselves that John Keats referred to when he wrote about living "in mystery and doubt without an irritable reaching after fact or reason"? How can we learn to trust our connectedness with the universe, whatever our mind, body, emotion, and other people are telling us? When will we learn how to care enough about our own happiness to focus on and trust good things rather than regretting and regurgitating the reality that we don't want?

Our inner being wants us to develop receptivity and willingness to honor our own desires. Contrary to popular belief, desire is nothing to be ashamed of. When we learn to listen to and live in harmony with our inner being we feel the peace and joy that comes from going *with* rather than *against* ourselves. We are in harmony with a universe that wants us to have everything. A universe that doesn't care if we have big desires or small desires or anything in between. But, let's face it, it is just easier for us to envision the little things because somewhere deep inside, most of us imagine that the universe is stingy and conditional. We think that we need to suffer and struggle our way toward what we want and that it is our suffering that qualifies us to receive good things. And while it is true that our suffering does illuminate what we really want, it's when we stop struggling, when we let go of our suffering, that we can fully open to the unlimited, all-connected space inside. And when we open in this way, when we become truly receptive to our nonphysical, inner source, when we are willing to trust something beyond our own thoughts and emotion, all will go well. We will feel bold and playful and not too stuck on the details or logistics. We will feel larger than our manifested lives—and we are. There is something easy and effortless about it. We know that everything will be all right. That's what it is to be in the flow. When we are in the flow, we stop contradicting our own desire. We no longer feel the need to make a case against ourselves. We love our life the way it is while at the same time trusting that what we want is good and the universe wants our happiness and fulfillment.

It all begins inside. It is energetic. And very straightforward. What we think about and the subsequent feelings we have about it is what we will bring into our lives. If we have negative expectations, we will have those confirmed. If we have trust and appreciation, joyful expectations and confidence, our lives will reflect that. It's annoyingly simple and yet every human being has a whole lifetime of proof of this. When we support ourselves and trust that the universe wants to give us what we want; when we feel good and our thoughts and feelings and subsequent energy aren't contradicting our desires, when we are tuned in, energetically, to our own desires, magic happens. All we have to do is to get out of our own way. We are here to be happy and learn or relearn how to trust that something, anything, can become available to us if we are willing to be still and non-regretful, openhearted and continuously assuming that our source wants what we want. All we have to do is welcome it with trust and confidence.

We are here to plant seeds in the rich soil of our own joyous bravery, our own trust and imagination, to water it and watch over it, knowing for ourselves without anyone else telling us that one day, as soon as our frequency fully matches our desire, something wonderful will come out of that soil. For most of us, this takes practice. The more we want something the more we tend to focus on the lack of it. But when we trust without tangible proof, we are an energetic match to it. And the funny thing is, when we learn how to be happy about what's coming, while at the same time accepting and seeing the beauty of what is, it's no longer that important whether we get what we want or not. But we will.

If you really pay attention to yourself, where you are on any given day, you will notice that life brings you exactly what you are reflecting. Just walk down the street. When you are feeling happy and joyful and generous, how do people respond to you? When you are irritable, stressed, and defensive, what is your experience?

Anne-Marie, a friend of mine, recently moved out of New York City to a house near her daughter's school. My oldest daughter goes to the same school, and one day we were planning on having coffee together after dropping off our girls. Only Anne-Marie called me right before and said her cat was gone. I came by her house with my dog, Arielle, so we could look for the cat together. "He was part of my heart," she said, "I am beside myself!" We had Arielle sniff one of the cat's toys and went all around the neighborhood and into the wooded area near Anne-Marie's house. I had a strong feeling that the cat would come back. Anne-Marie, while understandably moving in and out of despair about her missing beloved cat, was focused on trying to stay open to the idea of her cat returning. She met all of her neighbors during our little cat expedition. Many of them were sweet and supportive and promised to let her know if they saw or heard anything. A guy in one of the houses we went by said, "Well, there are coyotes in the area, and the big roads nearby. It's very dangerous for a cat to be out and about." "Don't even think about that, Anne-Marie," I said. "I don't mean to be insensitive, but this is not the time for us to worry about coyotes and highways, and soon we will be celebrating him coming back to you!" I still felt strongly that the cat would come back and I knew it was important to keep ourselves aligned with that idea rather than regretting the loss and fretting about the dangers. Anne-Marie was right there with me. She had already lost a cat in the city a couple of months earlier. But with this one, Anne-Marie said she had an intuition that he was still alive. We decided to put all our trust in the universe, stop looking, and go and have lunch. It was a lovely and relaxing lunch. We talked of interesting things, not at all limited to the missing cat. But when the topic of the cat came up, we just reminded each other that the cat would come back, and that all we had to do was to trust that and chill out. A couple of hours later, as I was leaving, I said to Anne-Marie "Text me when he comes back."

Later on that afternoon, just as I was leaving my house to take a walk with Arielle, Anne-Marie texted me to tell me that her cat "just ran up to the deck and meowed!"

I was not surprised but so incredibly happy for Anne-Marie and grateful to the universe for showing us both how it works.

The more we learn to trust that we are indeed here on this planet to find out how to live our lives in natural balance between our physical and spiritual being, joyfully trusting and co-creating with spirit in ways that have direct and tangible impact on our physical lives, the more we find ourselves in synchronicity with everything alive. We understand our part in all that transpires. And we learn that spirit is by our side, interested in the well-being and happiness of all that is alive.

The other day, I was doing some yard work, dragging fallen down branches and shrubbery from one part of our farm all the way at the bottom of the field in front of our house. I felt so tired. My legs had that weak, used up sensation and the whole effort was a battle between my body's wish to rest and my mind's obsessive desire to finish the job. When you live on a farm, or even just in a house with a yard, there is no end to the maintenance. I felt concerned about not having any energy. But then I decided that this was okay. And I thought about all the times where I have had boundless energy and how much fun it is to feel the energy circulating in my system, to feel strong and healthy, up for the task, enjoying the work to be done in the yard, connected with the energy of everything around me.

That night, I had that same traveling dream as the one recounted in the previous chapter. Traveling is a big theme for many dreamers. Moving from one destination to another, or trying to, is so central to most processes. This time, I was in a giant airport, with trains and subway systems connecting far apart gates. The system was complicated with trains coming on rails on multiple levels. Bewildered by it all, I asked a man with an old backpack if he knew how to get to my gate. He told me the number of the connecting trains that I needed to take to get there. As I listened to him I felt an incredible energy in my legs and lightness in my whole body and realized I didn't need the trains, I could just run there! The next day I woke up full of energy. I took a long run without feeling tired and got a lot of yard work done.

My point is, we co-create. We have the option to change the situation by not getting too caught up in limitation, past issues, and fearful anticipation. We can let our experiences point us in the direction of our desires. And if we can focus on a positive outcome rather than our fear and regret, vibrating authentically with what we want rather than what we don't want, we will see it show up in our lives. It is that simple and that complex. It is a natural principle and it never fails. We cannot fake it. Paying lip service to what we want while feeling disappointed and despairing about what is going on doesn't work. It's all energetic. And energy does not lie. Words alone are not enough. Energy created the whole universe. And energy creates our own individual lives.

There is a choice here. We can look back at our lives and think, "Oh, what a terrible life I created," "Dear God, let it not get any worse than this," "This really sucks," etc. Or we can make a conscious decision to focus on the beauty and diversity of everything. And we can zoom in on the present moment, while honoring everything that happened as our own roundabout way to clarify exactly what kind of life we want to move toward. And then we can start "vibrating" with that life, appreciating the path that brought us to this point. By vibrating I mean enjoying the idea of the life we have learned that we would like to have even before it comes to fruition. Knowing, deep inside, that the universe isn't here just to mess with us. We are part of the universe, and it is part of us, and there is no hell. There is us forgetting who we are and that can certainly feel like hell. But the truth is, everything is sacred and there is love in every corner of our interesting, multifaceted lives. And we are faced with never-ending opportunities to wake up to the sacredness of it all. And when we do, we are fully experiencing our heaven on earth.

Having a vision, and moving in the direction of that vision with the physical evidence not yet available to us, is the most fundamental part of any creative process, a necessity for our continuing evolution. To create our lives by trusting and enjoying that vision isn't just some vague, popular modern concept that people throw around to look interesting or successful. Having an inner vision, fostering the courage to trust and welcome one's dreams, one's inner knowing, has everything to do with being human. Courage and bravery, a willingness to act on internal instinct and inner knowing before seeing it in our physical lives, was what carried our African ancestors through the early challenges to human survival and is what ultimately determines how we progress and evolve today.

For many years, I had the pleasure of working with a wonderful man; kind, considerate, articulate, and honest. Let's call this client Michael. He was an actor in his late twenties, and while living in New York City he traveled all over the country working for local theaters, making an impressively stable income as an actor without having to take on a lot of side jobs to support his art like so many of his colleagues. But this tall, handsome, intelligent man had very little experience acknowledging any of his own accomplishments. He suffered major depression and told me that the only thing he looked forward to doing was lying on the couch in my office during his sessions, protected from the world around him—a world that he didn't feel he had the tools to deal with.

So he lay on my couch for a year or so, two or three times a week, describing his fears, finding brief relief from his agony, but mostly just remaining terrified and feeling like a failure. While not objecting to anything he described, I began to remind Michael of the foundation that he was indeed standing on, in spite of everything he was going through. In the beginning, we stayed with the facts. To do anything beyond that, to reach for vision and dreams, was going to backfire and make him feel like an even bigger failure. We reiterated the dry facts. We focused on his successes, on the days and weeks and months on stage where he was able to maintain a perfect equilibrium and an impressive form.

"What an interesting contradiction of your own beliefs about yourself," I would point out in the driest manner available to me. "How does a complete screw-up, an emotional mess, a total failure, somehow make it through hours and hours of theater, inspiring thunderous applause and theater directors hiring and rehiring him? If your character is so fundamentally messed up, why do your friends love your company, how come your family seems proud and invested in your well-being, and how is it that I, your therapist, rather than dreading our sessions, actually seem to enjoy our work together?"

Eventually, Michael was able to look at his accomplishments and know that they had something to do with him. He learned to trust himself so much that he was able to start exposing himself to uncertainty in a way he had never done before. Michael wanted to work in film and TV. He had no experience. Live theater was pretty much all he knew. But he eventually trusted himself and his inner vision so much that he was able to say no to going on tours across the country, and, without any guarantees, or stable salary, stay in the city and audition for the very shows and films he wanted to be part of the most.

His depression began to loosen its grip on him. He began to see he, himself, as the one who created what he wanted to create. He was learning to listen, rather than dismiss and criticize, his inner knowing. Gradually he began to actualize his dream, to work in the New York City film and TV industry. Slowly, he learned to trust that he had everything he needed inside himself to do whatever he wanted to do. He began to relate to himself with more respect and appreciation instead of constantly rejecting his own self-knowledge. He began to tune into his own instincts about everything from work to friendships to family and romantic relationships and spiritual awareness.

He became curious about himself. Little by little, he learned how to trust that he was complete, that he was enough, that he was trustworthy and worth listening to. And most important, he began to feel less like a fraud and more alive. He began to experience that there was a real and true vital and vibrant sacred space inside himself that connected with everything around him. He laughed more. He made jokes. First about himself. Then about me. Then about everyone and everything in his life. He started dating more regularly. His romantic relationships lasted longer and became more committed. He was increasingly open about being gay. It seemed less and less important. What was important was that he could feel his own aliveness. His own love and power to have influence over his own life.

> *Anything you want to ask a teacher, ask yourself, and wait for the answer in silence.*
> —BYRON KATIE

As all this was happening and Michael lost his diagnosis of major depression, it became clear to him that he no longer needed me. He was right; there was nothing more that I could add to his life. There never really was, the answer had always been inside him. He just had not always known that. Or, as my daughter Elsa put it, in the spring of her eighth year on this planet:

Elsa: In the light of speech, life concocts a
   remedy!
Me: Hm, where did you hear that?
Elsa: I just thought it
Me: Yeah? Do you know what it means? Cause
   I'm not sure I do.

Elsa: Yes, it means if you tell yourself you can do
    something, you can. You can choose what
    you are.

I know she is right. And yet, one may wonder, why is it
that so few people actually live in awareness of these
choices? There's no easy answer to that question. I do
know however, that when we learn to understand the
wholeness of things, the beauty and value of every experience, one illuminating the next, we have the clarity we
need to move toward a more actively creative life where
we see clearly the choices and the freedom that our lives
offer us from the moment we wake up, throughout our
day, all day, every day.

Take Carina, for example. A smart, interesting woman
in her early thirties. When she began working with me,
she had crippling anxiety, frequent panic attacks, depression, and regular incidents of self-injury, cutting herself.
She was an economics student, well spoken, a quick
thinker and very entertaining as she constantly, in spite
of her anxiety, joked about everything, including her
own acute anxiety. She had that going for her. But she
still was a mess. She cried and ranted, was on and off
antianxiety medications, very unsatisfied with herself
and therefore, subsequently, deeply unhappy with her
environment. She studied hard and was still sure it was
all going to fail and that she would never graduate and

never pass her exams. In spite of her emotional struggles, something inside her was stronger than her doubts, and she did manage to get through school and passed every one of her exams with flying colors. She attained a position as a human resources director for a big firm. Because of her strong conviction that she wasn't good enough for this job, she eventually got fired. She had a powerful experience of being wrong. We looked at this in therapy and she eventually saw that this experience not only contributed to her getting fired but caused it.

She got another job. At this point, Carina was ready for things to go better. She began to learn not just to respect her own professional abilities, but also her time away from work, her right to rest and not make everything about living up to the expectations of her employer. She began to become aware of her right to well-being. She went off the antianxiety medication. The panic attacks subsided. From having been caught in a vicious circle of constant overeating, mostly junk food, and too much alcohol, too often, she began to take an interest and pride in taking care of her own body and eating and drinking mindfully. She joined the gym and started swimming. She began to listen to her own dreams, literally and figuratively. Her night dreams were often about expanding, discovering a new space within herself, finding more personal freedom to live her own life in whatever way she wanted to. Her daydreams, similarly, were becoming less about fear and failure and more about her own desires. She talked about how she wanted to live in a small house with a vegetable garden. How she wanted to travel and how she enjoyed her life with a handful of very close and supportive friends and had no desire for kids or husband or a conventional life. We worked on the idea of supporting her own inner knowledge about what was right for her and recognizing that the only potential obstacle to the manifestation of those things was her own unwillingness to support her own dreams.

Our sessions became less about what other people did to her to make her miserable and anxious and more about what she could do for herself to get closer to a stable and continuous sense of well-being. The quality of our conversations changed dramatically. From therapy being a place where she vented about overwhelming and out of control feelings of anxiety and rage, Carina began to express a kind of low-key confidence that was originating inside her rather than being determined by what happened on the outside. As Carina herself said one day recently:

"Even though I don't have everything under control, things are okay."

She stopped making herself wrong about everything. She began to listen to her inner voice, which told her that everything was okay, even when she didn't yet have full, external evidence of that. And when she did relapse into anxiety and stress at work, she noticed how her anxiety made her want to lash out at one of her clients or coworkers.

The difference was, she could see these tendencies without judging herself. And since she didn't judge herself for it, she no longer had the need to justify her feelings of discord. She observed them more and acted on them less. And she stopped using them to contaminate her time away from work. She learned how to just observe the discomfort of those old feelings without getting so stuck in the adrenaline of it all. She no longer had to make everyone, including herself, wrong. She was beginning to trust that her own basic nature was good, regardless of what feelings came and went.

Pema Chödrön, in *Taking a Leap*, writes:

> *Our resentments and self-centeredness, as familiar as they are, are not our basic nature. We all have the natural ability to interrupt old habits. All of us know how healing it is to be kind, how transformative it is to love, what a relief it is to have old grudges drop away. With just a slight shift in perspective, we can realize that the people strike out and say mean things for the same reasons we do. With a sense of humor, we can see that our sisters and brothers, our partners, our children, our coworkers are driving us crazy the same way we drive other people crazy.*

Becoming more forgiving and accepting of her own feelings, her own experience, Carina's internal environment, as well as her relationships and professional experience, transformed. Instead of her thought processes feeling tight and riddled with fear and anger, she began to experience herself as more relaxed and spacious. And in this spaciousness, she could hear the voice of her own desire more clearly. She could begin to think about her own life in a new way, where everything was much more accessible, much more possible. She was beginning to understand in a very real way that she was not so much a victim of her circumstances as she was the creator of them.

Impossible is just a word thrown around by small men who find it easier to life in the world they've been given than to explore the power they have to change it. Impossible is not a fact. It's an opinion. Impossible is potential. Impossible is temporary. Impossible is nothing.

—MUHAMMAD ALI

Few athletes have been more inspiring to me than Muhammad Ali. He had the kind of joy and confidence that simply cannot, in every sense of the word, be beaten down. He just knew his own greatness. And he spent years holding onto his own conviction, nurturing it, being faithful to it, playing with and enjoying the idea of it, not just when it became clear that his inner vision was becoming reality, but uncountable training hours before that happened. He wasn't just talking. It wasn't just a bunch of grandiose words about how he was going to be great. He lived by it. He believed it. He enjoyed the thought of it. And he refused to argue against himself. And the universe listened and gave him the wings that allowed him to fly, in the exact way that he had asked for it.

Many great men and women have accomplished wonderful things that we all benefit from through their willingness to know without yet having any physical evidence of their knowing. The world is made from the kind of faith that is what Khalil Gibran referred to as "knowledge within the heart, beyond the reach of proof." Or, in Albert Einstein's words: "I believe in intuition and inspiration . . . at times I feel certain I am right while not knowing the reason".

In a way, you could call the men and women, girls and boys with this kind of indestructible vision magicians. They know and evoke what the eye cannot yet see. They focus their energies on what they want in such powerful ways that it becomes true. So it is in the proverb about the villagers praying for rain. "On the day of prayer all people gathered, but only one boy came with an umbrella. That's faith."

Most people have experienced periods of their lives where faith and trust just seem like lofty, unattainable concepts that have nothing to do with them. There is a sense of complete disillusionment and a feeling of being disconnected from themselves, other people and the universe, lacking confidence in their inner vision or deprived of that vision altogether. Some call that depression. Others are so familiar with that place that they call it life.

Not too long ago, I had the pleasure of working with client in the music industry. Don was a deep feeling man who struggled with being overwhelmed by his emotion. He started therapy because his girlfriend, the mother of his only child, had cheated on him. They separated but were intricately entangled in a love-and-hate relationship that was debilitating to both of them. My client was a prescription drug addict, and when I stated this (to me somewhat obvious) fact, he was so offended that he took a break from therapy. When he came back, he was in an even worse shape, having started to combine his prescription drugs (antianxiety, antidepression, antipsychotic, and sleeping medication) with alcohol. The picture was bleak. Don's relationship with his girlfriend as well as with his young daughter was getting worse and worse. He was so tortured by anxiety and depression that he was suicidal most of the time. I told Don that I didn't think figuring out his past would help him resolve his life. One day, things were so terrible that my client finally agreed to get substance abuse treatment.

He started going to substance abuse groups as well as working one-on-one with a substance abuse counselor. For a while, we paused our sessions. Eventually Don was stable enough to reengage with his life, restart his therapy with me, improve his relationship with his daughter and ex-girlfriend, and refocus on his work. Later that year, he went to Europe and had a powerful experience by the ocean. He was hang-gliding and below him was a large number of dolphins. He asked the person holding onto the ropes to lower him and he was lowered so far he was able to glide along the surface of the water together with these beautiful and intelligent water animals. The experience had a powerful impact on Don. It spoke to him about boldness, presence, and freedom, and a sense that absolutely anything is possible. He had witnessed an incredible kind of bridge between his inner knowing and physical reality. It made a long-lasting impression on him.

A little while after this trip to Europe, Don was ready to end our work together, with the idea that he could come back if he wanted to at some later point. One day, a year later, he called me, complaining bitterly again about the latest shortcomings of his ex-girlfriend in a custody battle that had recently flared up with renewed vengeance. We scheduled an emergency appointment.

I listened quietly for a while as Don elaborated on his disagreements with the mother of his child, the woman he had once been so deeply in love with.

"Do you want this to be what your life is about?" I asked him.

"What do you mean?" he said, slightly annoyed.

"You have enough fuel here to last you for the rest of your life. You could keep hating this woman and be engaged with her in this way forever. Nothing much would change about that part of your life. You could keep throwing more logs on that fire. Or you could let your life be bigger and freer than that."

"What am I going to do about this? It's my daughter, I have to protect her!"

"I don't buy it. I don't think this is about you protecting your daughter. I hope you don't mind me saying this, but I think this is about you not separating from your ex. You are still as intimately involved with her as you always were. Only now it's a negative involvement. Remember when you swam with the dolphins? The miracle of that? Why would you choose to live this small, powerless life when you know you are capable of opening up to experiences like that?"

My client looked at me, half annoyed, half intrigued. I continued my little rant.

"You are an artist. You like to live according to your vision. When you don't act on your vision, what you know is possible makes you miserable. You are meant to be free."

Don stared at me for a long time. His eyes became glazed over. We sat there quietly for a long time. Finally, Don broke the silence:

"I know what you mean."

He stood up and walked toward the door. I followed him there, neither of us saying anything. Then he hugged me, tears streaming down his face. That was the last time I saw Don.

"Courage" Maya Angelou says, "is the most important of all virtues because without courage, you can't practice any other virtue consistently."

It takes courage to believe in things we cannot see and to go to places we haven't known about before. Many people are not accustomed to using the kind of courage that it takes to trust things that are not yet evident. We don't celebrate until we know for sure. We struggle with trusting that everything is going to work out and just keep on engaging with what is, no matter how miserable and limiting. We are a little bit like Toad in *Frog and Toad Together* by Arnold Lobel. Toad follows his friend Frog's example and plants some flower seeds in his own garden. As soon as he had planted the seeds, he started talking loudly to them:

"Now seeds, start growing!"

As the seeds did not immediately show up, Toad moved closer to the soil where he had planted the seeds just minutes before, shouting:

"NOW SEEDS, START GROWING!!"

As nothing happened, Toad figured his seeds were afraid to grow so he read a story to them, he lit candles to keep them happy, he sang songs, read poems, and played music for his seeds and got increasingly discouraged and annoyed when he could see no proof of them growing.

Truth is, we don't have to do all that. Some seeds may grow better if we just hold our own intention, our own desire, in our own heart and leave the seeds alone, free to grow in their own time. We don't have to rush anything. Push for anything. Struggle. We can let go of our efforts but still hold on to our desire. We can trust that what we want is good and what is good will work out for us. We can just know that we are doing the best we can to be open to having a good life and let good things in and that everything will be, and already is, just fine.

The idea is that finding what we want is something much easier and softer and more natural than most of us have learned to believe. It's less about thinking it through and finding cognitive solutions and strategies as it is about receptivity and openness. It does not have much to do with rightness and wrongness. It's not a fight that we have to win. Life is not meant to be a war-zone. It's beyond the struggle. It's about what we find when we have tried everything and we begin to understand it's not so much in trying and doing as it is in being. We just need to slow down enough to notice what we already have and who we already are and allow it to flow through us.

The idea that the solution is in the connection with everything is, of course, not at all new. But when someone at any point in human history devotes their life to this trust and receptivity rather than to individual strivings and struggle, there is always revolutionary change. There is something very powerful on the other side of agenda, individuality, ego, control, fear, suspiciousness, needing proof, demanding that something compensates us for our lack of faith. If we truly want to connect to that universal power, a part of us—the controlling, struggling, fighting, evidence-hungry, manipulating, strategizing part of us— has to get off the center of the stage. If we truly want to find, we have to be willing to lose. Well, we don't have to, but we can. We can learn to lose in a trusting way. In a joyful, confident, free, and open way.

There is a secret power in being able to laugh whole-heartedly before we have proof that our manifested life supports that joy. We can laugh and smile and chill the things we want into existence. We can do our rain dance and trust, like so many before us, that the sky will respond. We have so many opportunities as humans to jump, visualize in the dark, know before knowing, and let go of our desperate, white-knuckled holding on to all that we consider essential and real. We can do all this before finding what we are looking for and learn that a truly free and harmonious life comes without conditions. And, as if that freedom and harmony isn't enough, it turns out that our unconditional life, our joy and inner knowing regardless of circumstances, comes with incredible abundance! We have every reason to learn how to joyfully honor our inner knowing rather than letting our current reality distract us away from our vision. We have every reason to take our eyes off the challenges that we are facing and listen to the love and creative power inside ourselves. That love can erase any obstacle and create any miracle. There is no limit to what we can have and do when we are in harmony with and connected with our own inner being. That connection, wherever it is allowed, whenever it's honored, makes everything new. Mother Nature illustrates this astonishing power in the most convincing ways.

In the nature documentary series *Our Planet*, one of the episodes focuses on forests. The narrator, David Attenborough, describes Mother Earth's response to the accident in the Ukrainian nuclear plant in Chernobyl. This accident is among the largest man-made disasters of our time. And yet, against all predictions, after almost one hundred thousand people were evacuated from the area around Chernobyl after the catastrophe, Mother Nature made an astonishing comeback. While humans were gone, the forest grew back and wildlife was exploding in a time span of only three decades. The endangered Przewalski's horses started to roam around the now-desolate city. Suddenly, there were seven times more wolves inside the evacuated area than outside it. Brown bear, lynxes, bison, moose, over two hundred bird species, and many other species found refuge in the area and the forest was and is thriving. It is speculated that the human influence is so much more dangerous for forest and wildlife than the extensive radiation in the aftermath of the nuclear disaster. With or without radiation, if given a chance to thrive, Mother Nature's resilience is remarkable.

The same is true for us. When we are willing to go beyond our calculated thought processes and agenda, beyond trauma and hardships, beyond our individual selves, allowing ourselves to become quiet and slow down enough to listen internally, anything is possible. Aligned with our source, we can become powerful thrivers and creators. Not only can we recuperate from life's challenges and setbacks, but we can learn to live joyful and satisfying lives just like Mother Nature did in one of the worst disaster zones in history.

Mother Earth shows us so many things about how to live. She is willing to win and lose and know that everything is a prerequisite for everything else. Her willingness is evident through every new season. There is no other way for new leaves to grow than the old ones dying. Death is not death. Death is life. The end is the beginning.

If it's true, and it is, that we are part of everything and everything is part of us, what is there to fear? What are we lacking? Regretting? If we are both the problem and the solution, why worry? If darkness and light illuminate each other, why prefer one to the other? We are much more beautiful, large, limitless, connected, and complete than we think.

> Dear tree,
> I watch you
> All year
> Willing to be beautiful, colorful, and naked
> Willing to lose it all,
> exposed to cold winds and ice
> only to burst out of your seams
> once again in spring
> Help me be like you
> Help me win and lose
> Without preference
> Help me Die
> And be Born
> Help me Stand
> Quiet, Open
> Full and Empty
> Help me Welcome
> Everything

So how do we cultivate this inner knowing in our everyday life? How do we become creators rather than victims? How can our lives become like the forest around Chernobyl— resilient, lush, a refuge for others, diverse, alive, and constantly expanding, regardless of circumstances? I think the answer, somehow, is much too simple for most people. We overintellectualize and overcomplicate most matters. We are set in our beliefs that the answers are either outside ourselves or up in our heads. And we think the answers are most likely to be highly complex. Only accessible to us through endless sacrifice. Through excruciating effort. Painstaking analyses. But the truth is, we are so much closer to what we want when we chill out and stop obsessing about it. When we loosen up our contracted muscles and become open, spacious, and receptive. When we find silence. This is when we start getting inspired. This is how things begin to flow freely through us—effortlessly, naturally, instantly. When we are this allowing, this receptive, we are beginning to channel the whole universe.

Or, as Alice Walker said,

> *Helped are those who create anything at all, for they shall relive the thrill of their own conception, and realize a partnership in the creation of the Universe that keeps them responsible and cheerful. . . . Helped are those who lose their fear of death; theirs is the power to envision the future in a blade of grass.*

6

Intention and Magic

*Let yourself be drawn by the stronger pull of that
which you truly love.*
—RUMI "THE ESSENTIAL RUMI,"
TRANSLATED BY COLEMAN BARKS

IT IS NOT easy to explain the things we don't see. In the
Western world, for the most part, whatever cannot be
proven in a linear, concrete fashion is not taken seri-
ously. Magic is often a dismissed concept. It's ridiculed,
belittled, deprecated, underestimated, downgraded. It's
more like a party favor, a frivolous, extracurricular

parentheses rather than something that is accepted and validated in our daily lives. It's even considered dangerous and depicted as something that, at best, shows up in horror movies, is associated with the devil or negative, harmful forces. It's thought to be something that only a shady and unstable person would associate with. And of course, unreliable and questionable characters have exploited magic and ritual motivated by revenge and anger. But the most life altering magic, the truest form of it, derives from love. When we open up to magic in ways that respect the natural laws of the universe, it can be extremely powerful in very positive ways. Magic in the service of love is dignified and worthy of attention. It is light, uplifting, and reliable. It is trustworthy and incorruptible.

In the shamanic world, power and magic are often called upon through observing and learning about the ways of the animals. In many shamanic cultures, for example, the raven carries the medicine of magic. The raven is present in many Native American healing circles, across the United States. It brings healing and clearing of intention, and can remind us of the magic of being alive and how to properly use our energies. I have always loved wild birds. Ravens, in particular, remain playful and totally unfazed by the most challenging situations. They aren't intimidated by strong winds and rough weather. And they love to play in the middle of the toughest conditions.

Some years ago, my two girls, their father, and I went to Minnewaska State Park Preserve in upstate New York for a couple of days of hiking away from busy New York City streets. We took day hikes in the beautiful mountains while slowly letting the intensity of the city melt away. One afternoon, Elsa and I sat in a little gazebo placed right at the edge of the mountain facing incredible views. As we watched, a large bird flew in our direction. It had the wingspan of an eagle but as it came closer, we realized it was a raven. It flew right toward us from a mountain peak. As it came closer, I began to feel uneasy. It began circling right above the little gazebo. Round and round it went. The unease I felt about the raven's interest in us gave way to a sense of magic. I felt, and Elsa felt, that this very large, beautiful, pitch-black, wild, playful creature brought us good news. We were both so happy about this meeting and knew that it would leave us freer and help us open up to magic. And as we returned back to the trail to find Tony and Lina, Elsa detected a shiny black feather on the ground. We brought it home with us to remind us of the magic raven, its playfulness and raw, beautiful fearlessness.

Magic is in everything, whether we recognize it or not. It is what draws two people together through unseen forces and makes them inclined to join each other in such a powerful way that it creates new life. Magic works alongside instinct and intuition, informing a receptive mother of how to hold her baby and what sounds to make or words to say or tunes to sing to envelop her baby in peaceful, happy states. Magic makes us find our path and our loves and our passions. It helps us find our pets in a shelter full of barking dogs. There is that one dog that looks at us in a way that captures our heart. There is a sense of connection and pull that makes everything quite simple and obvious. Magic lights up our path so that we can find our true north, our soulmates, even after what seems to be decades of relationship mishaps. Only none of those other relationships were mistakes. They were just the stars on a cloudless night, leading the way. Our lives are full of magic and when we truly acknowledge this simple fact, we notice synchronicities everywhere we look. We become open to a whole new language, a source within speaking to us through animals, nature, numbers, words, synchronistic events, all day long. All that is required in learning this beautiful, sacred language is openness and receptivity.

Magic helps illuminate the hidden. When the secret and the hidden find expression, everything can change. What is hidden wants to come out—that's the power of life. Magic shows us how truly connected we are with everything alive. And if we open our hearts and minds to this simple fact, we will never be bored or disheartened again. Or, in Rumi's words: "Stop acting so small. You are the universe in ecstatic motion."

When we stop arguing for our disconnectedness, our lives become one never-ending alchemical adventure. The practice of alchemy, which originated in medieval times, is based on ideas of transformation of various materials, most specifically converting base metals into gold or other universal medicinal or magical potions.

In more general and modern terms, alchemy can refer to any process of transformation and creation that we cannot explain in concrete and tangible ways. The way I have come to understand it, everything alive is part of an alchemical process. All life impacts something else, leading to transformative and creative processes. There is ongoing change and movement everywhere we look. And the more we look, the more receptive and still we are willing to get, the more we learn about the magic that's all around us.

> "The world is full of magic things, patiently
> waiting for our senses to grow sharper."
> —W. B. YEATS

The way the snow falls quietly outside our window, muffling the sharpness of every sound, may have something to tell us about how to soften and become more receptive. Or maybe it speaks about innocence or simplicity or starting over again. Every message that you become aware of, every alchemical process that you are part of, is unique to you and your relationship with your inner spirit, which, in turn, is connected with everything around you. Once you allow yourself this connection, you will just know it is so. And you will learn to recognize that it happens when you are in a peaceful, still, and receptive inner space. It very often happens during or after meditation. In nature. After a storm that left you very quiet and very clear.

You may know somewhere inside you that the particular hawk circling above your path, along the road that you are driving one day, is relevant to you. It may remind you to be observant, take a higher perspective, pay close attention to what's happening at that moment, or to what you are doing. Or it may encourage you to listen to your own intuitive awareness about something. You may suddenly see frogs everywhere in your path. Those strange little creatures hopping up to your house, sitting around on the roof outside your window, may remind you to be content with what is, or to slow down or let go of something that no longer serves you and make room for something new. Signs and symbols will come into your awareness, over and over, until you get the message that is meant for you. The frozen ice needles, sometimes referred to as diamond dust, may remind you to trust the beauty or purity or clarity of something in your situation. The bees that keep coming into your sphere, building their hives outside your house or up in your attic, however annoying or bewildering or inconvenient, may remind you about the sweetness of life, the beauty of collaboration with others, the joy, balance and sense of connection that comes from true reciprocity. The pink sunset that lights up everything after an almost inconceivably difficult day; the hard rain that you felt inspired to walk right into, letting it wash away every ounce of regret in your whole being; the slippery road that made you take a turn that brought you to a special place that you had never seen before; the soft wind touching your cheeks, letting you know all is well; the tears on the cheeks of a stranger; the warm, knowing glance in a moment where words are superfluous; the reoccurring colors, reminding you of a very happy feeling; the friend you haven't spoken to for years who calls you seconds after you suddenly thought of them; the lost internet connection that recharged your creative process and reminded you what it was you wanted to write when your internet connection was restored; the reoccurring numbers that relate to something or someone specific in your life; the canceled trip that saved you from an airplane crash; the dying relative and the way you intuitively saw it coming so that you could go there and see them one more time before it happened; the opened doors that led you straight to someone that had something very important to tell you at the exact right moment; the coyotes yapping away that one night after a day of everything in your life was turned on its head—none of it is outside that genius puzzle that constitutes our alchemical lives. All of it is grace's messages to us. Every breath that we take is magical. All is love and sacred synchronicity. There is never a wasted moment. Not even one.

> "The work of magic is this, that it breathes and at every breath transforms realities."
>
> —RUMI

Most scientist agree that a large part of our universe does not play by ordinary, traditional rules. This part, referred to as dark matter, cannot be understood in the logical, methodical ways that we have normally use to investigate and predict things in our world.

According to *Live Science*, "Dark matter is a mysterious non-luminous substance making up the vast majority of matter in the universe. Though experts have observed the gravitational effects of dark matter for decades, scientists remain baffled as to its true nature."

The website of the European organization for nuclear research states that "unlike normal matter, dark matter does not interact with the electromagnetic force. This means it does not absorb, reflect, or emit light, making it extremely hard to spot."

In *Scientific American*, "Dark Matter May Feel a 'Dark Force' That the Rest of the Universe Does Not," the idea is presented that dark matter may be interacting "with itself through some unknown force other than gravity that has no effect on ordinary matter."

In other words, there is matter in the universe that cannot be explained by the laws of physics. It's undeniable that there are vast portions of the universe that we don't know much about. Some scientists assert that dark matter has no influence on what we consider ordinary matter. Others suspect that this unknown force actually has a strong influence on the structure and evolution of other matter, including us! The idea in the case of the latter argument is that just because something is hard to detect, and even though we are unable to analyze it with traditional scientific tools, doesn't mean it lacks impact.

Generally speaking, science is gradually opening up to concepts that don't comply with what we traditionally consider to be universal laws and truths. Throughout history, however, individuals, groups, and cultures who have had the courage to trust the things they couldn't see, and purposefully interact with those things, have often been harshly punished for their beliefs and practices, not only ridiculed and condemned but often also captured, imprisoned, and even killed. The Salem Witch Trials in Massachusetts were hearings and prosecutions of mostly women accused of witchcraft in the late 1600s where more than two hundred people were accused, thirty found guilty, and nineteen executed by hanging; it is one of many such tragic and fearful responses to things unknown. I believe that we need witches in the world. More than ever, we need women and men who are connected to the whole, capable of seeing beyond their intellect, willing to see beyond ego, profit, convention, and limitation.

To deny and reject magic is to deny and reject ourselves. Because we *are* the magic. It is not outside us. It is part of us and part of everything.

It has often been asserted that we use only around 10 percent of our brain's capacity. Similarly, I think it's safe to say that most people live most of their lives with just a fraction of an understanding of just how incredible and magical our lives, our universe, and everything in it really is. When I was very young, I felt the true magnificence of everything alive, and I had a natural and egoless understanding that I was part of all of it. I felt sure of my own ability to transcend sorrow and limitation and to channel the love that I knew was inside me and everywhere around me. I felt that I could extend peace to someone who was terrified and bring a kind of simple clarity to someone who was caught in confusion. I felt that love could travel through me and touch those with deep sorrow, shame and loneliness. I felt sure that love was really the only thing that truly mattered in life and that love was powerful and anyone who wanted to be touched, transformed, and enlightened by love was warmly welcomed. I spoke to fairies in the forest, felt the energy of little stones and big rocks, and didn't think that the stoic wisdom of the trees all around me was something I was not allowed to know about. I felt the potential of everything alive and the excitement of being part of the alchemy of life. I understood, instinctually or spiritually, or maybe magically, that in order to survive and be who I was meant to be, I had to spend a lot of time alone in the quiet mystery of the forest.

There I listened to something other than words and concepts, learning about how to live and breathe with confidence and trust, regardless of circumstances. I understood that life is much more than I could conceive of with my five senses. I also understood that sorrow and limitation and hidden matters could be transformed into joy and possibility; that nothing was static, and that love and light was the birthright of everything alive. In this way, I felt protected by the whole universe—which to me at that time consisted of the forest and the lakes, the trees and the waters and the wild and domestic animals in the countryside where I grew up—and the love and magic that I perceived all around me.

Our lives, and us in it, are so much more miraculous than most of us have words for. I don't think this is something anyone can fully describe with words. Our ability to perceive this magnificence stands in direct relationship to our ability to understand that we are one with everything around us. If you look at images of brain cells and compare them to images of galaxies, you will see striking similarities. Or, take the microscopic image of the birth of a cell and compare it to an image of the death of a star. You are likely to be blown away by the resemblance. If you need more proof of your connectedness with the entire universe, take a close-up look at an eye and compare it to the helix nebula (the planetary nebula located in the constellation Aquarius). What do you see if not an almost shocking mirror image?

Sure, we can live our whole life in denial of that inside and outside ourselves that we don't fully understand. We can we live entire lives oblivious to our interconnectedness. We can go on staring at the tangible and trust nothing but the evident. Or, we can get curious. We can wake up to fuller, more interesting, more deliberately transformative and creative lives. We can open ourselves up to magic in more purposeful ways with the understanding that we are energy beings, connected with all life. We can direct our energies in service of the greater good, aligned with our source, with our higher selves, with spirit that lives inside us. In a purposeful, deliberate manner we can become part of transformative, protective, clearing, and attracting processes. Inspired and guided by love and love alone, we can have very deliberate impact on our own lives and sometimes on the lives of others.

Guided by love and purposeful intention, we can give birth to new life, literally and figuratively. We can clear energy, move energy, create new energy and transform already existing energy. We can have direct and intentional influence over the progression of our own lives. We can align with the sunrise and the new beginnings in the East; the completion and the releasing, protective and illuminating energies of the West; the fluidity, the fertility, and abundance of the South; the authentic, expansive, new pathways of the North. We can become so receptive and so quiet and still that we become and act as one with our own source and with all things alive. And that is what it is to wake up.

How do we tap into magic in more intentional, deliberate ways? Sometimes, I think the storms, obstacles, and losses in our lives that can feel very destructive and terrifying at first can open the pathways toward the things that we otherwise may be too busy or distracted to recognize. Upheaval of any kind can have a cleansing and clearing effect on us.

When my girls and I first moved to North Salem a few years ago, Lina was going through an extraordinarily rough time and after one particularly difficult evening, I went downstairs to the living room where Elsa was sitting and reading in the middle of the storm. I walked over to the living room window, staring out into the dark night, tears streaming down my face from pure exhaustion. Elsa looked up from her book and over at me and said, "Mom, when everything is destroyed, what's left is the only thing that really matters." And that's how it worked with us. Sometimes, a storm was the only thing that could help Lina release her anguish and pain. And somehow, those storms not only released her challenges, but those of the rest of her family as well. Those storms were so extreme that they cleared the air for our whole family. We were all affected by the maelstrom and all released by it. With our intention to emerge freer, with more love for ourselves and each other, those storms often ended up having a liberating quality.

We learned, gradually, to direct Lina's episodes of frenetic energies, which often felt very destructive at their onset. We learned to take advantage of the turbulence, the calm after the storm, the new insights that came along with the many ways that autism continually turned all of our lives upside down. We found positive changes, new awareness, new growth, and renewed love and understanding for each other at the end of every hurricane. In our own individual ways, we all found ways to use those energetic upheavals as possibilities to open ourselves up more. We learned to value the opportunities and to accept the losses of whatever had been destroyed in the storm. And we came out freer, bolder, more loving and somehow more fully human and awake on the other side.

And so, it may turn out that the hurricanes and tornadoes that we worry will wreck all that we value in our lives, only take from us what is in the way of our freedom. Through these cataclysmic events, we may be liberated from our normal sense of what's believable, what is normal and what isn't, what is expectable and appropriate and customary. We may end up with greater awareness, an expanded openness to something so different and so much more interesting than the usual fear-based, codependent conformity that kept us trapped, miserable, and confused.

But of course, we are not deliberately going to create upheavals to gain more awareness and openness to the things that we cannot see. That would be destructive. The most concrete and deliberate way to open ourselves up to magic is the very opposite of upheaval. In stillness, life begins to illuminate itself to us in ways that we may not have thought was possible. When we are still, quiet, and willing to put our intellectual, emotional, and even spiritual pursuits aside and simply listen, magic automatically happens. We will see and hear things that we never saw and heard before. We will understand our connectedness with everything alive and in seeing this interrelationship we will understand that we are not here to be victimized by circumstances but rather to be co-creators of our own lives.

I know that this can sound like a simplistic cliché. But if you have felt your own presence, beyond your own thoughts, beyond attachment and agenda, in that quiet space where everything is just right, you will know about the magnificent possibility of all things. For me, there is no other way to connect with who I really am than to quiet down. When my head is full—when I grasp for things that I want, worry about things that I don't want, try to figure out my life or my feelings or my thoughts— whatever I'm focused on multiplies. And the process goes nowhere. Or, rather, it goes round and round in unproductive or exiting circles.

Only when I let all those things fade into the background can I connect with the wholeness of who I am, my true presence, the infinite aspect of my being that's not the slightest bit compromised by any part of my experience. In this connection, I fear nothing and see only love and possibility. In my experience, this usually starts up as something better described as vibration rather than a bunch of insights. And that vibration, that state of feeling whole and untroubled and open, is all anyone ever needs. It's a place in its own right. It's complete in and of itself.

But while that is so, somehow that place is also only the beginning. It's really the empty, decluttered room where magic and miracles can happen in more direct and deliberate ways. In this high-frequency state, we are truly receptive. And that is all that's necessary for positive change and liberation, or whatever it is we hope will occur.

Receptivity is the beginning of all good things. It's really not some great mystery. On a purely relational, interpersonal level, in our physical lives, receptivity is always the one thing that rectifies even the most difficult relationship. It is always the one ingredient that establishes or reestablishes even very unlikely or troubled connections.

So naturally, the same is true for our own connectedness with our inner being. We connect in the moment we let go. We experience ourselves—our source, our inner, infinite being that is connected with everything alive—most powerfully when we are still and receptive. And when we are in this connection, anything is possible and everything feels clear. And not only does it feel clear and possible, it feels good!

As you stay here, you may have an idea about something. It may seem as if it just came to you, effortlessly. And that's exactly what happened. You didn't have to struggle to attain it. It just appeared in your mind. And you know it's right, because it's an idea that is in total harmony with every aspect of your being. Or, you may have an impulse to do something. Or you notice something profound that's been in the dark for you for a very long time. Maybe you saw it when you were a child but when you got older you lost it, or forgot about it, or suppressed it. Suddenly you may have crystal clear understanding of something that was muddy and confusing just before. It may feel like one epiphany after the next. You may smile.

You may feel really happy to be alive. You may feel a kind of excitement and lightheartedness and incredible calm and confidence that makes you eager to continue your day or talk softly to someone you love. You may hear yourself saying to the spirit within—thank you.

Finding this place of peace and connectedness becomes the beginning of your co-creating in more and more deliberate ways with all that is. From here, no one has to remind you to be present or loving or grateful or to look at the bright side of things. No one has to tell you to chill out or energize yourself or love your life or your neighbor or your husband or your work. You no longer need someone to tell you they love you and you don't feel the stress of trying to get more beautiful or in better shape. You don't have to search for any more proof that life is worth living or that you will get to a better place in your career or relationship. In the moment you connect with who you truly are, you realize that you have every- thing you need and that you are part of a creation that knows no limits. You realize that *you* are the magic. You don't have to go look for anything at all. You are already everything you need. You are already there.

7

Silence—A Gateway to
Our True Self

P ABLO NERUDA, IN his poem, "Extravagaria,"
describes how in the willingness to slow down, "a
huge silence might interrupt this sadness of never
understanding ourselves. / Perhaps the earth can teach us."
Mother Nature is a powerful teacher of silence and
stillness. She models for us how to be alive and moving
and growing and yes, expressing ourselves and being
exuberant too, but without meaningless and unnecessary
noisemaking. She moves with purpose and dignity. Her

pulse is slow and calm. She has so much power, and she will use it if she needs to, but her basic MO is generous, non-demonstrative, still, and quiet. Her silence as well as her expressiveness heals us.

When I moved out of New York City for good, it was to live in North Salem, a very quiet little town in northern Westchester, surrounded by nature preserves and inhabited by eagles, coyotes, otters, occasional bears, foxes, ravens, and many other wild, powerful, and wonderful creatures.

A few years into this "going back to the country" endeavor, I realized that I couldn't picture ever moving back to a loud, busy place like New York City. I did live happily in many busy, loud places for decades. I slept through angry rantings on the street outside my bedroom window, fire trucks, ambulances, police sirens, and groups of loud, drunk teenagers shouting and laughing. The first day I came out to North Salem, after the moving guys had left, I noticed the silence. Though I grew up in the country, there were decades and a lot of city noise between my childhood and me. As I now found myself in an empty, quiet house in the country in my early fifties, the silence seemed less than peaceful. It seemed to almost exacerbate, or rather, illuminate, the noise in my own head. Truth is, that first night in the peaceful countryside, was not the slightest bit peaceful. I didn't sleep at all, not even a blink, that first night. And

I thought, "What have I done?" Why had I dragged my kids and myself out of all that was familiar, away from all our friends, all that we knew, all that we were used to, to a place where we knew no one, where I had no clients, no routine, suddenly living on a farm that needed so much work, so much attention, that if I spent the next ten years trying to fix it up, it would still scream out for more?

These questions were not answered for a good while. But gradually, I began to focus on the goodness of this move. A few months into our country living, the silence began to feel healing and soothing rather than purely aggravating. Slowly, I began to appreciate the stillness. As the days went by, our house, and the trees and grass and birds and bunnies and coyotes around it, became home. Silence became my refuge rather than a reminder of my own and everyone else's neurosis. Silence became my friend, my remedy, my bliss.

Have you experienced the silence of snow, softly falling? The snow muffles and dulls the sharpness of all sounds and forms and touches the ground quietly. Snow often represents rebirth and purification. When we learn to truly listen to and watch for something other than the sound and the form of things, we become aware of our own purity and that of everything alive. Silence and stillness are not just the absence of speech and noise making. It's beyond moving, trying, making an effort and having an agenda. It's listening to our own being, beyond all that we have become accustomed to define as ourselves.

Stillness is about letting go of all attempts. It is to just exist in the center of everything, without doing anything. And in this stillness, we find a kind of vitality that has nothing to do with our age and physical health. All the power in all the world comes from here. The answer to the riddle of our lives is not found by looking for it. It's not something we *do*. Our searches just lead to more searches. Endless searches. Lifetimes of frustrating, backbreaking, heartbreaking searches. Only when we sit down in the middle of our lives—open to everything, radically accepting of every nook and cranny of our psyche, of every sensation in our complex sensory system, of every sound inside and outside ourselves and every impulse running through our bloodstream, every thought passing through our mind, without holding onto or chasing after any of it—can we find our own powerful, silent, pure presence.

Here is the answer to everything. Here, in this vast silence and space, in what seems so inactive but is so full of everything, there is no need for answers. Here, all is obvious and abundantly clear. It doesn't have to be discussed. There are no words to describe it. It doesn't have to be processed. It cannot be processed. It is not compulsive and obsessive, it's conscious.

In *Dhammapada, The Sayings of Buddha*, the truth is found when we quiet our mind and "come into that empty house" and "feel the joy of the way beyond the world."

Buddha spent a lot of his life in silence. Through his inquiry, he recognized that he had everything. He was full. Silence is full and satisfied. Silence is not trying to attain anything. Silence and stillness is not about anything. It's about nothing. When we try to better ourselves, when we look for more, improved, deeper, shinier, we are focused on the lack of it. When we want something and think and talk about what we are missing and what we don't have, our thoughts, whether we say them out loud or not, make a lot of noise. We scramble around on the surface of things, getting louder and more restless, frustrated, unsettled, and dissatisfied. When we surrender to nothingness, to silence and stillness, we find everything and that everything, we come to see, is us.

When we are silent and still, we find ourselves beyond the superficial and underneath the surface. And we understand that we are beyond life and death. We see that there is nothing we have to try to achieve in order to survive. It is something we are already. We can become conscious of this or live oblivious to it. It doesn't matter. It is there, regardless.

When we open to silence, the universe, our source, God, spirit, grace, our true self, whatever you call it, interrupts our sadness and fear. A deep, wordless under-standing takes the place of our old paranoid and depres-sive, confused and limited, ideas about ourselves and our lives. What had appeared hurt, compromised, corrupted or even dead in us comes abundantly alive and whole.

When we are truly quiet, we can hear everything. In this space, we find the purpose of life. We find grace. Here is the unlimited, the sacred and the whole. And we understand that our universe and everything alive, including ourselves, are part of that core, that purity. There is no greater discovery. It changes and illuminates everything. We become astutely perceptive. We can hear our own breath, and the breath of others, beyond the sound of it. We can perceive our own heartbeat and the heartbeat of others. We realize that our pulse is perceiv-able too. In our silence a whole new dimension opens up to us.

Our perceptiveness expands and expands along with the space that we allow into our consciousness. Gradually, we learn to hear something that isn't so much a sound as an energy, a frequency. We know what is close to us, not just physically, but in other ways too. We can sense the frequencies of other people, and eventually those of ani-mals and plants too. Distance and time begin to matter less. We can perceive not just what's physically near us, but also that which is farther away. We can become aware of what is coming into our sphere and what is on its way out of it. We can experience things, tendencies, energies, frequencies beginning to happen or beginning to subside. And we can notice ourselves opening or closing to it. We can observe conflict and fear without being pulled into it. As this silence and stillness become central in us, we can talk and move while being quiet and still. We talk less and the words we use are less noisy.

We are encapsulated by the most acutely perceptive silence and vast peace. Our lives change. We begin to perceive things with the ears and the eyes of our inner source of light. We find ourselves sitting in the middle of our own heart. And the heart of the entire universe. This is where love has no beginning and no end. It is in this silence that we find ourselves the most fully awake. It is here that we finally find the meaning of life.

8

Inspired and Awake

N OW AND THEN, we have the joy of getting to know others, both people and animals, who have a natural ability to live in free-flowing, joyful, and creative ways. They make everything they do look so easy. They welcome life in all its variety, they know what to hold on to without much effort and what to let go of without much regret. They are not at war with themselves. Without even thinking much about it, they acknowledge and trust their own inner vision, regardless of circumstances. Most importantly, they are not fundamentally nurtured and inspired by outside rewards and acknowledgment and proof. Their power comes from their connection with their inner being. And their inner being is connected with the entire universe. The natural consequence of being connected in this way is a sense of limitlessness. An experience of lightheartedness, openness, spaciousness. A sense that things are working out and flowing with ease—calmly, joyfully, without struggle and tension. And with this flow comes inspiration. And with inspiration comes creativity.

ELSA

How do I know that the ground needs a kiss? I'm kissing it.

—BYRON KATIE

"Miracles dance on the edge of eternity and in the breath of life, waiting to be perceived by our wide open eyes."

—ELSA

She was about eleven years old, and in the middle of one of her graceful twirls, when this sentence flew out of her. Elsa is my youngest daughter. She is an independent. She has her own thoughts and her own values. She is a deeply happy person, someone who seems to have somehow figured out how to live at her optimum most of the time. I realize this must sound quite exaggerated coming from her mother, but she is the most harmonious person I know. She finds joy and excitement in every single aspect of her life. She spends a lot of time every day reciting things that she is happy about. She reads a lot. She can be unbelievably silly. And her seriousness is potent and focused but very rarely severe or heavy. And while she can be private, with many things that even her best friends don't know about her, she doesn't actively hide. She is actually strikingly transparent.

She metabolizes her feelings quickly and intensely, getting angry in an obvious, honest, and straightforward manner, and then she lets it go, as if it never happened. But the truth is, people just end up wanting to be good to her. She is so true to herself and seems to have so much clarity about what works for her, what she can endure and do for others and what she cannot endure and is not willing to do. Her no is just as solid as her yes. And as her mother, I find it hugely reassuring that someone with so much love and compassion has those boundaries in place.

She loves people. Some years ago, when Elsa was still a little girl, I went to the beach with her. It took her less than five minutes to find a friend. When it was time to leave, I looked up to see her standing with a family of seven, all of them holding hands, looking out at the ocean together, Elsa's pale body and yellow hair in sharp contrast to every member of the warm, large African American family that she had made collective friends with.

If you were to ask me what she looks like, I could tell you, well she has long curly, intermittently brown and blond hair and freckles in the summer. She has a heart-shaped face and a dancer's strong back, strong arms, strong legs. She has a little nose and a mouth that's often shaped in a smile. She kind of looks like a little fairy. I'd always thought that as she got older that fairy look would subside but somehow, as I'm writing this, she is nearly sixteen, and it's still there.

When Elsa was eight years old, I watched her playing soccer on the schoolyard with a bunch of boys. One boy kept passing the ball to her. I was impressed. Many boys prefer not to pass the ball to a girl. Not this one. I made some kind of comment about this to her after the game. She recognized it and concluded that the boy may have passed the ball more readily after she had climbed up on the tall fence that surrounded her schoolyard to take down the boy's backpack. One of the boy's classmates had thrown it up there as a joke. "Why did you do it?" I asked Elsa. "Well, it was very hard to get to. He needed it," she responded matter-of-factly.

We talked about Jesus around the time Elsa was in second or third grade.

"You know how Jesus died, and took everyone's sins upon himself?" she said to me one night right before bedtime—the time of the day when Elsa almost invariably turns into the philosopher. "I think Jesus kind of had the wrong idea about people," she said and looked straight at me to gauge my reaction.

"How so?"

"Well, if people do something bad, if they sin or whatever, that means they don't feel good about themselves, and that's the main problem."

"Oh yeah?"

"Well, you see, if they feel fine about themselves, then it doesn't really matter if they did something wrong in their life. Nobody is perfect. They have to forgive themselves in order to be happy for the rest of their lives. But if some random dude, however nice and interesting, comes around and says oh, guess what, you have really messed up your life, but I can fix that. I'm gonna die and take all your sins with me. That's not really going to work."

"Why wouldn't that work?"

"Well, I imagine that he thought that by taking away their sins he would make them happy but really if they can't forgive *themselves* they are not going to be happy. What I mean is if Jesus can't forgive them, but if they can forgive themselves they are still going to be fine. But if Jesus forgives them and they can't forgive *themselves* they have a problem. Jesus of course was a very kind and inspired person but in a way he didn't trust that people could figure things out for themselves and that was a kind of judgment so he wasn't completely perfect. I am sure he was very kind and wonderful, and often very misunderstood, but maybe he didn't always think through completely how he was going to be helpful to people."

There is nothing gullible about her. She isn't easily fooled. She sees her fellow man in all his contradictions and shortcomings. She sees right through people, and she loves what she sees. The human. The limited. The defensive. The irrational. The beautiful. The whole. She sees it all but instead of being pained by it, she is fascinated and intrigued. It's endearing to her. All the stuff that makes up a human being touches and moves her. She doesn't take it personally. She sees the complete, overall picture. She somehow has the perspective to recognize the fear or the frustration or the desire that led to the behavior and just accept it for what it is—humanity.

When Elsa was nine years old, we talked about Maya Angelou's poem, "I Know Why the Caged Bird Sings." She said, "I think what Maya Angelou meant was that people can feel trapped sometimes. But by embracing the things you wish and hope for, inside you can be free."

Elsa has learned her spontaneous and unquestionable acceptance of people from her sister, Lina. At the time Lina first regressed into autism, Elsa was a year and a half old. From then on, Elsa watched her older sister transform from a calm, charming, verbally skilled, and unusually generous and inclusive big sister to someone who was thrown into immense challenges and incomprehensible tornadoes. During all the years following this traumatic turn of events, Elsa observed her sister's struggle through sensory mayhem, uncontrollable breakdowns, loss of words, and oceans of confusion, sorrow, panic, and disintegration. She saw her sister regaining lost ground only to lose it again, a few months later. She saw Lina having seizures and Elsa celebrated with us when the seizures began to subside. She witnessed Lina being trapped by OCD and anxiety, her difficulties leaving the house in the morning and her struggles with settling in at night, and Elsa celebrated every one of Lina's triumphs, connecting with friends, writing her first essay, shooting hoops, riding bikes, and expressing her real thoughts on the letter boards.

Lina and Elsa somehow preserved their love and respect for each other through every setback, every difficult transition, every new obstacle in Lina's way. Elsa joined her big sister in listening and singing along to her every favorite song, whether it was Yo Gabba Gabba's "It is fall it is fall, the leaves are falling everywhere, that means it's fall" or Maxwell's "Pretty Wings." She patiently looked forward to less challenging times while embracing every ounce of joy that she could detect in the moment. She loved her sister through thick and thin, darkness and light, sickness and health. And Lina loved her right back, from inside her tornadoes.

In all of the ups and downs of life in our family, Elsa seemed so strangely capable of preserving not only her compassion and patience, but her happiness too. The more challenge, the more vibrantly and passionately she seemed to express herself in her dance lessons and performances with the National Dance Institute (NDI), and in her writing and creative play, and later at the Alvin Ailey School of Dance and at the Ridgefield Conservatory of Dance.

Elsa reminds me of a woman described by Pema Chödrön in *The Wisdom of No Escape*. In the story, the woman is chased by tigers.

> *She runs and runs, and the tigers are getting closer and closer. When she comes to the edge of a cliff, she sees some vines there, so she climbs down and holds onto the vines. Looking down, she sees that there are tigers below her as well. She then notices that a mouse is gnawing away at the vine to which she is clinging. She also sees a beautiful little bunch of strawberries close to her, growing out of a clump of grass. She looks up and she looks down. She looks at the mouse. Then she just takes a strawberry, puts it in her mouth, and enjoys it thoroughly.*

And that's how Elsa went through her days during the tough years, her mouth full of strawberries, tigers above and below.

When Elsa was a middle-school preteen, I started to wonder (like every other mother, I'm sure) where is she going? Who is she going with? What will her life be like? Will she be caught up in all the things that won't matter much when life gets complicated? Should I worry or trust that she will find her own way?

One day, she and I talked about how the purest joy comes not from praise and rewards, fame and publicity and acknowledgements on the outside, but from something deep inside that connects with everything that is. I knew she already had this one down, but somehow, she heard it in a way that she hadn't heard it before. There was a shadow crossing Elsa's face as she instantly realized that she, in order to be happy, had to give up everything that most people hold on to for dear life. She was pretty quiet for the rest of that afternoon. The next day, in school, she wrote this poem:

The River
Will you teach me how to flow
Freely, unbound
Over the piercing rocks
Will you show me how to breathe
With the pulse of the earth

Can you stretch out your hands
To me, like you do
To the stoic mountains
Can you wear out a path
For me to walk upon
I will take your hand
And follow you
Into the vast ocean
I will fall into your gentle arms
And pour into the sky
Can you let me float downstream
Like you do
To the fallen oak leaf
Can you give me
To the beauty of the earth
Will you teach me how to dance
Without looking
Behind me
Will you show me how to leap
To let go of the ground
I will sing with you
Until my voice
Is gone, like the sun sets
I will laugh with you
Until my throat
Is bare and hoarse
And I will dance with you until

Like you
I am free.

—Elsa H. Lyons

When I was young, growing up in the Swedish country-side with forest and lakes all around me, I felt a very deep connection with nature and the wild animals around me. Moving out of New York City after Lina and Elsa had become teenagers, and again living in an area with a lot of wildlife, this connection has been reestablished for me. Sometimes, as a tool to focus in on the teachings of the natural and animal world, I utilize a kind of animal tarot cards to clarify, channel, and understand things better.

At the end of 2020, I was doing one of those guided meditative inquiries about Lina, hoping to gain insight into her current experience in light of all the challenges we had been through together over the fifteen years since she regressed into autism. The vulture card showed up. The significance of the vulture is often misunderstood. It is commonly seen as representing death and destruction but really, rather than destruction it speaks of the connection between life and death, the idea that nothing is ever wasted, all is sacred, and all our challenges and suffering can be transformed into wisdom and understanding, fertilizing the very ground we walk on, becoming the fuel that lifts us up and helps us find our higher ground.

I talked with Lina about this idea in the middle of the night, as she was having trouble sleeping. I reminded her, just like the vulture had reminded me, that nothing is wasted, that her experiences have enriched all of our lives, and that the vulture represents a higher, freer perspective, pointing toward the blessings and sacredness of everything. She of course already knows this, but she enjoyed hearing it nevertheless and eventually fell asleep. Elsa was fast asleep in a different room when Lina and I had this conversation and knew nothing about the vulture message. A couple of days after this late-night talk, Elsa woke up with a dream. She said she didn't quite know if it was a dream or something else, as it felt very real and vivid.

Elsa's recollection of her vulture dream:

> I was standing in a big field, leading a few different people in a sort of guided meditation thing, based on these two different hypothetical interpretations of seeing vultures circling overhead. There were a specific number of vultures—two of them circling. In one interpretation, the person takes the vulture as a bad omen, of death and doom and stuff. Then a family member of theirs dies and they think the vultures referred to that.
> In the other interpretation, the person sees the vultures and is filled with enthusiasm and

inspiration and begins to shout that death isn't
real! Because a vulture eats dead animals, and
those bodies then become the new matter of the
universe!
Then a family member of theirs dies, and they
think of the vultures and are filled with relief,
because they no longer believe in death.

And that's Elsa. Uncanny and relating naturally to her
higher power through her close connectedness with
Mother Earth.

One day, driving home after one of our daily hikes, we
saw some deer wandering into the woods next to the
road. It was getting dark and pretty cold and Elsa, a little
bit concerned, asked me if deer lay down and sleep at
night or if they always just walk or stand around? I
responded that I think they probably do sleep lying
down, but that I'd never seen one sleeping or resting. The
next morning, I was driving Lina to her school in
Rockland. Elsa was still doing every other week at home
via Zoom classes, and just came along for the ride. Before
I brought Lina to her school, I dropped Elsa off by a
little wooded area nearby so that she and our dog Arielle
could have a little fresh air and movement before getting
back into the car for our next stop.

When I came back to pick up Elsa she told me that
she and Arielle had just had the most beautiful

experience. They had come to a little open space in the wood and had seen three deer laying down peacefully in the grass. Arielle had not made a sound, and she and Elsa had just stood there, watching the resting deer who strangely didn't seem at all bothered by the onlookers.

And that's how Elsa creates, in close synchronicity with Mother Earth, asking and receiving, open to abundance, clarity, and inspiration wherever she goes.

"A house overgrown by ivy is like the earth reclaiming everything," she burst out from the back seat as she and Lina and I were driving by a house one October afternoon. From the decayed look of it, no one seemed to have lived in it for many decades. For Elsa, everything that happens seems to be a sign that things are working out beautifully. The lock down, to Elsa, became the greatest opportunity for her to be with me and Lina, liberated from having to drive around to all the places away from home that we normally drive to: the city, school, dance classes, friends' houses, and more. While she naturally missed her dad, this time was Elsa's chance to practice and learn how to plan discussions and communicate on letterboards with her sister. It was an opportunity for us all to hike for hours every day. We had time to study, play, work out, laugh, and cook and read together, on our own terms, without the constant interruptions of the outside world. It was incredible to have Elsa at fourteen, and Lina at sixteen at home for three full months without having to bring them anywhere else.

And Elsa's enthusiasm over this opportunity never seemed to subside. She loved every new idea of how to utilize our time, what to study, what books to read, what food to eat, what trail to hike on. We made a little movie. We wrote poems. We studied every nature preserve, every trail, every mountain and lake and forest in the area. Elsa and Lina were the perfect lock-down partners. Hanging out with them during those months and what eventually became more or less the whole year of 2020, was like being back at the university again. We studied various poets and tried to write in the style of that poet. We read Richard Adam's *Watership Down*, Jack London's *Call of the Wild*, Yann Martel's *Life of Pi*, Anna Quindlen's *Still Life with Bread Crumbs*; discussing, comparing, reflecting. We talked about living and dreaming, how to perfect our raspberry scone recipe, psychology and anthropology, future husbands and what to study in college. We shot hoops, hit the speedbag, did planks, and climbed mountains. We set intentions, and learnt to understand ourselves and each other a little better. As everything slowed down around us, we found a little more connectedness and clarity. Elsa started writing poems every time we took a hike. This one is called "Alchemy."

The universe is an alchemist
It makes me out of strange and precious materials
It makes me a shapeshifter,
Gives me all the forms
Sculpts me out of fire water earth and air
And whispers truth into every particle.
So I say let us open the gates
And let the rivers rush down
And drink the rain and water the peach-tree with
our tears
Let us be Taoists
And anarchists
Let us be nobody at all.
Let us grow long, long necks
And look over the tops of our thoughts
Then let us begin again
Let us bathe in the night sky
And dry in the light of the sun
Define nothing, and welcome everything
Understand nothing, but know everything.

Elsa is clearly very happy with who she is. But there is
nothing arrogant about her. She is humble, honest, authentic, exuberant, often self-mocking, very rarely demonstra-
tive, and almost never defensive. But she loves and accepts
herself deeply through ups and downs, highs and lows,
rain or shine. Her devotion to herself and her family and

the specifics of her own life, as well as the rest of humanity and Mother Earth and the entirety of the whole universe, is a stunning constant with her. The other day, right around the new year of 2021, she wrote an ode to herself.

Ode to Myself

Lion—girl
You are abundant like the buffalo
You twirl like Fiery-colored leaves
You are eternal.
Every inch of you is a flowing river
Springing out from the earthly source
You are waves of water and sky
You are wind.
You recognize yourself in the beaming sun
And also in the breathtaking full moon
So the entire sky
Is your mirror
You ride on the backs of
Galloping constellations
You are held in a cocoon of light
The night and day carry you
Trees sing you lullabies
How could you ever be alone
When you are nothing more or less
Than the essence of the universe?

MEHARI

Faith is a knowledge within the heart, beyond the reach of proof.

—KAHLIL GIBRAN

Mehari Gebre Medhin was born in Eritrea in 1937. He is a Swedish-Eritrean pediatrician, nutrition-physiologist, and professor of international child health. For most of his professional life, Mehari worked as an attendant at the Children's Hospital in Uppsala, Sweden, responsible for overseeing acutely ill children. He came to Sweden as a young man and got his medical degree from Lund University in southern Sweden. Upon his graduation, Mehari immediately went to Harvard for a master's degree in public health. Only a couple of years after Harvard, Mehari attained a PhD in Uppsala, where he still resides.

I met Mehari through my mother, whose older sister, Anna-Greta, worked as a missionary in Ethiopia (now Eritrea) and became very close with Mehari's family. After Anna-Greta was killed by a robber while being driven in a taxicab in Ethiopia, my mother adopted Anna-Greta's interest in Ethiopia and close family ties with Mehari's family. My mother had some of her happiest years with them before reluctantly returning to Sweden to study music and teaching.

Mehari and his brother Ezra Gebre Medhin moved to Sweden in their early adulthood, married, and had children. Their families and my mother's two other siblings and their families remained very close. Their kids became my cousins. As a young child, when someone pointed out to me that Mehari and Ezra's kids didn't look anything like me and my brothers and couldn't possibly be my actual cousins, I just thought they were wrong.

Mehari taught me about God with words that were unlike any I had heard before. He freely mixed Christian concepts with some not-so-Christian ideas about God, or whatever I wanted to call it. He talked to me about God being limitless and inside everyone, and about how we can live our lives influenced by that awareness. Rather than focusing on the idea that we were all sinners in desperate need of forgiveness and redemption, Mehari spoke about how we, as well as every other living creature, had a vastness and an expansiveness inside us that we could tap into and that would make our lives much more interesting and miraculous if we allowed it. And because of that, we should live full of faith and joy, Mehari pointed out in the slow and methodical way that he spoke, because we are not really separate from God, we are part of everything, and because of that there is nothing to fear and nothing to worry about.

What I remember most about Mehari, and what is still true whenever I see him on one of my rare trips to Sweden, is his confidence. It goes well beyond the boundaries of his own person. He appears to always have an expectation that everything is going to be all right. While he defines himself as a Christian, his concept of God is broader and more inclusive and all-encompassing than that of any Christian I have ever met. His trust in a benevolent God, in spite of all the suffering he has encountered both in his homeland and in the intensive care units for children in Swedish hospitals, is unquestioned. Mehari never imposes his beliefs. He just utilizes those beliefs to be a better friend to everyone he comes across. To me, as a little girl, I remember how safe and calm it felt to have him around. Everything in life seemed brighter when Mehari and his family were in our house. My mother was always happy during those visits. My father, too, brightened up significantly when he had a chance to laugh and talk and relax with this tall, dark-skinned man who always seemed so together, so curiously unfazed by all the madness around him. He had a vision for his fellow human beings that wasn't very detailed. And it was never imposing. It was more a kind of a "live and let live" vision, a sense that everything would be okay, that he was able to carry not just for himself but for everyone around him.

In my early twenties, I used to hitchhike from Gothenburg, where I lived, to Uppsala, where Mehari lived, which, under lucky circumstances, would be a seven-to-eight-hour trip. It was unquestionably worth it for me to hear Mehari talk about life and living from that entirely different perspective than I had grown up hearing. To me, there was nothing better than to sit around the table in the home of Mehari and his loving wife Susanne and eat delicious pasta dishes with heavy-cream tomato sauce that Susanne had made to help fatten me up. Food never tasted as good as it did around Susanne and Mehari's dinner table. During this period, I was thin as a rail and not sure how to keep on living my own life. I felt that I had somehow missed the memos about how to get by in a world that seemed so heavily bogged down by misery. I still remember my relief when, after many hours with strangers in various cars, I saw Mehari's little white house among rows of other little white houses. It was a simple row house, nothing about it was particularly impressive, and yet, to me it looked like a castle. It symbolized home. Safety. Love.

While waiting for Mehari to come back home after his work at the hospital, I'd walk around Uppsala all day long, looking forward to the time before dinner when I would have an evening walk with Mehari. I had never met anyone before who seemed so sure that everything would work out. He seemed so unimpressed by the challenges and obstacles of everyday life. And he related to everyone and everything in such a bold, cheerful, consistently kind and gentle manner. Mehari always talked slowly, weighing his words carefully. He listened quietly, and when I challenged him on his idea that everything was going to work out for me, he related to my objection with the same nonreactive, evenhanded patience as to anything I might say that was more aligned with his own philosophy.

Only once have I seen him troubled. It was in the morning, and the end of one of my many stays with him and his family. I was getting ready to go back to Gothenburg and wanted to start early as to avoid having to hitchhike after dark. Mehari said he wanted me to come with him and have a little snack at a café in Uppsala before leaving. He wanted to talk to me about something.

"Helena," he said as we stood around waiting for someone to show us to a table, "you know you're always welcome here and Susanne and I always like to have you around."

"I know, I feel that, thank you so much for having me."

"It's our pleasure." He looked at me and seemed to be weighing his words extra carefully. I was getting nervous. What had I done now? What was wrong? We sat down by a little table near a window.

"You know Helena, we all have things that we need to work on, things that hold us back, things that makes life harder than it has to be."

I couldn't disagree about that. I had a lot of such things, a never-subsiding list of things that I had to work on, that held me back, that turned my life into an endless struggle.

"I would like for you to let me pay for your train ticket rather than you hitchhiking."

"Thank you so much. I really appreciate it, but I cannot let you pay for that. It's enough that I come here and you guys help me so much. I just can't let you do that. It would just be that I cannot come then, hitchhiking is the thing that I can do to make it possible for me to go back and forth."

"It would make me very happy to pay for your tickets. I am in a good position to do it. But when you hitchhike, I worry about you. That's not working for me. Sometimes when you let someone help you, it's a gift to them."

"I am already giving you a lot of those kinds of gifts."

"Yes, but you have a lot of catching up to do in this area."

"Yes, but I am giving the people who pick me up the gift of picking me up and driving me."

"Yes, but your hitchhiking here to see me does not work for me."

"Then I'm afraid I cannot come here."

"Then I'm afraid we have come to a fork in the road."

I stared at Mehari. He did not look cheerful. He did not look like he was going to light up the dim café with one of his infamous smiles anytime soon. The idea of him paying for my ticket every time I came there made me cringe. My

instinct told me it's a terrible idea. It looked like the beginning of the end of my respite. But letting Mehari pay for
my train rides was beyond what I felt I could do.

"Helena, I am taking you to the train station."

I looked at him. He was still serious. He was not going
to budge. I could see that. He was not interested in my
opinion on the matter. I could see that too. He knew I
was dying in my chair. He thought of it as an opportunity. He thought that this part of me dying would make
my life better.

We left the café quietly. We drove to the train station
without saying much. I cried on my way there. He
bought the ticket to Gothenburg, handed it to me, and
walked me to the train. It was not until the train started
to move and all I had to do was sit there that I realized
how relieved I was that I didn't have to hitchhike. It was
not until there was no more room for me to protest, to
do it the way I had always stubbornly insisted on doing
it—to reinforce the idea that I didn't need anyone—that
I could breathe, really breathe, with the relief of letting
someone else take over.

When my biological father died, I cried about losing a
father who I didn't really know in the arms of the one man
who taught me everything I knew about what it means to
be a father. Mehari was my father when I was looking for
one. He showed me life on the other side of town. The
brighter side of town. By doing that, he helped me in three

major ways. He taught me my first important lessons in loving what is. Accepting what comes to me. Allowing life in all its imperfect perfection to nourish and sustain me. He showed me how to let things flow. To let things come and go. To forgive my family for their difficulties showing their love, to accept love when it came to me in all the different forms. And to know, deep inside, that everything, no matter what it looks like on the outside, is okay.

ARIELLE

She is how I know that the Universe loves me.

Her confident swagger the first day she came to us, tripping through the gate and up into the house as if nothing was more obvious to her than living there with us.

The one quick bark outside the door when she wants to come in. Her trusting eyes and willingness to just sit there and wait until someone acknowledges her request.

The way she stares out the window at the smallest outside noise to make sure there are no intruders by the gate, thinking, no doubt, that she, the little runt that she is, could do something about it if there was.

The little happy sighs in the middle of a cuddle.

Her reckless sprint right into the pasture of my friend's unpredictable, tough-guy alpha horse, settling for licking his nose through the fence after I managed to capture and drag her out of there.

The way she lives how she wants to live, fearless, bold, oblivious to her own size, just as happy about the real as about the imagined, sharing her love wherever she goes, ready to play, or kiss, or eat, or get admired, or chase a friend, or take a nap at a moment's notice, ready to be distracted from what she is doing, ready to keep on doing what she is doing, ready to get into trouble, ready to be.

She is here. And if there is one thing that we in modern society struggle with, it is that. Being present. Just being in the only space truly available to us—the now. Someone recently said to me that dogs are already in paradise here on earth. I think some of them are, the ones we respect as living beings in their own right, rather than subordinates we are here to dominate and whose main purpose for being here is to satisfy our need for love and obedience. I think the most meaningful, beautiful, and satisfying relationships between humans and animals, wild and domestic, as with every relationship, are the ones that are built on mutual respect, receptivity, equality, and humility. We know so little about the animal world. We have so much to learn. And in the process of trying to understand an animal, any animal, domestic or wild, we almost invariably end up learning more about ourselves than about them.

Arielle is a mixture of Staffordshire terrier and American bulldog. She originally came from a breeder but ended up in a variety of situations without success and finally came to us through a friend of our family. This friend was one of Lina's teachers from when she went to school in the city. He happens to be very knowledgeable about dogs and instinctively thought this dog would be perfect for our family. He called me one day, asking me if I wanted to come by to meet a four-month-old puppy who somehow had ended up in his house after a number of unsuccessful placements. Lina and Elsa and I met her briefly on a basketball court in Yonkers the next afternoon. She was extremely active and very friendly and happy-go-lucky. Later that night I drove back and picked her up for good. She hopped up in the car without hesitation and settled in on the front seat next to me for a nap. Back home, she strutted through the gate, played around on the grass outside our house for a while, and trotted into the house to acquaint herself with what she appeared to immediately perceive as her new home. She slept through the night in my bed, squeezed between me and Elsa, sighing and snoring and scooting as close as she could to both of us. She showed no signs of anxiety about any of it—eating sleeping, playing, and napping as if she had been with us for her whole life.

I don't know what she was thinking and feeling, but I suspect she knew even before I did that she was going to stay here and that this was her home. She has made our lives so much better and richer and more fun and interesting, and I hope we do something similar for her. Her expressive eyes and endearing face, the way her ears flap in the wind when she runs, her sweet kisses, her small stature but mighty personality, her interest in and love for people and curiosity about every little shift in the wind, every scent, every new sound, is so appealing and inspiring. She is her own dog, her own being. Compared to who she is, I have so little to teach her. My pragmatic little rules and regulations are so silly compared to her vast, natural intuition, the way she reads energy in us as well as in strangers, the way she steps up to the plate when she is needed and asks for help when in need.

It's an incredible partnership, mutually beneficial, always evolving. It's constantly illuminating things from the nonverbal world, the things beyond words and calculated, manipulative thought process. She teaches me about herself, about what connects us and disconnects us, about what she enjoys and what overwhelms her. I know now that when she comes over and sits on my feet she can use my help and some extra support and protection. When a dog she doesn't know comes running toward me, she feels that it's her job to intervene and protect me. She wants to observe the other dog and make an assessment, before letting them come close to me. I know which other dogs are great matches for her and which dogs intimidate or annoy her. The way she is with other people teaches me not just about her but also about them. The way she is with me helps me understand myself.

I love watching her. It never gets old, because she is always right there, in the middle of her life, exploring the earth, endlessly hopeful and joyful, finding all kinds of trouble out there on the open field in front of our old house, letting out little sweet sounds of pleasure as she stretches out her small but muscular body in the sun on the wooden porch, or jumping up, racing over to the couch, leaping up, and pouncing down like a miniature leopard on the little that's left of the stuffed toy that I threw there seconds before. Her expectant sprints into the kitchen, tail wagging, ready for breakfast as I let her inside after her morning pee, the way she rests her strong jaw on my upper arm or shoulder on cold winter nights where no amount of closeness is too much for her, the variety of sighs and snores and snorts and deep, happy breaths and swallows and dreamy smiles are all miraculous reminders of her incredible presence in my life. I never get tired of any of it.

Without intending to, she opens my heart and draws me deeper into not only *her* world, but mine as well. Without effort, she helps me become more available not just to her but to myself too. She is a living heart-opener. Without trying, she makes everyone smile. Her natural, non-manipulative, sweet, and trusting presence, makes our home more of a home. She teaches us how irresistible and recommendable pure, unselfconscious presence is.

Having someone around who trusts that good things are going to happen to her, who accepts life and other beings as they are, who regrets nothing and expects everything, who doesn't pine for joy but lives in the middle of it, raises the vibration of everyone around her. She is the embodiment of someone who knows, on a deep instinctual, visceral and tangible level, that she is already everything she needs to be.

Afterword

When I questioned what I believed about reality I came to see that reality is much kinder than what I believed it to be.

— BYRON KATIE

PABLO NERUDA, IN "The Sea and the Bells" (William O'Daly translator) describes the non-dual nature of the world. "If each day falls inside each night," he wrote, there is "a well where clarity is imprisoned." Clarity exists. Our days and nights, our darkness and light, life and death, all of it, is here for us to open to and embrace. In the well that is our soul is our freedom, our infinity, and our limitless love.

Recently, my oldest daughter Lina was attending an astronomy class via Zoom. At the beginning of the class, Lina admitted that some of the thoughts about the vast cosmos, the incredible planetary system that we are all part of, made her anxious and left her feeling overwhelmed. I didn't know enough about the solar system to be either intrigued or bewildered. But as we took this beautiful class together, taught skillfully and empathically by Lina's Eurythmy teacher, Elsa McCollough, I noticed in myself a growing sense of connectedness with the heavens. And Lina became more intrigued than bewildered. Going out with Arielle at night for her last pee became a time of awe. Looking up at the stars or checking out the shifting shapes of the moon began to feel more and more magical and, at the same time, as if this whole thing—this incredibly beautiful vast, glittering, star-sparkling space—had something to do with us! That it was, in fact, our home! And that home connected with a sense of being home inside. And that feeling of both vastness and familiarity inside illuminated the unlimited and infinite possibility of all that is alive.

Ultimately, I wrote this book to remind myself of the things that I, in the middle of being human in the life that I live, sometimes forget. I am hoping that some of those reminders, or new ideas as they might be for some, may be helpful in allowing a feeling of being a little more at home in the world, awakened to something beyond the habitual and mundane that feels uplifting and freeing and joyful and bold. It is my wish that some of those ideas will facilitate and deepen an understanding of what we are doing on this particular planet and how truly vast and unlimited and expansive our lives can be. And I'm hoping that you can discover and read between the lines or through the lines of this book that you are loved, supported, and fully cared for by the universe. That, contrary to what we often believe, this is indeed a benevolent, kind universe that we are not separate from but part of. And as we wake up to this unity with everything alive, we will find our own and everyone else's joyous, bold and fearless power to create lives that we are happy to have and to share with all the living beings around us.

You may still wonder, what does all this have to do with me? My life, my mortgage, my nine-to-five, my distracted husband, the political chaos, my habitual, familiar, anxious thoughts? My disillusioning past experiences?

It is not easy to let go of the habit of staring down the reality we find ourselves in as if it is fixed and unchangeable. We are not used to living from the inside out, trusting what we know deep inside that is beyond logic, limitation, and separation.

But we have an ongoing invitation to accept the notion of magic and infinite possibility. We are eternally welcome to come to the edge and see beyond our own limited assumptions and discover the space that knows no boundaries, that sees only peace, joy, unity, creativity, and love. The door is always open to the space inside ourselves that does not need to heal, where

everything is possible, and nothing, absolutely nothing,
is lost.

My Strange Friend

Walking along the water's edge
Feet waking up to soft soil
covered in pine needles
Roots and rocks along the narrow forest path
Sun streaming through leafless beech branches
Pure gold reflecting its playful power in glittering
water
Where an Ibis is floating
Strange looking, with its long, awkwardly curved
beak
Thin neck and white wings with a splash of steel
blue at the center
The catapulting power of those wings
nonchalantly reaching for . . . everything
for East and West
North and South
Air replacing water and earth
A tentative friendship is formed
Between soft soil and blue sky
It is now
It is trapped or free

I take a leap and jump up on that disproportional
creature's back
my earthly preoccupations blown away by breath
and wind
Each flap of this unusual being's wings
coinciding and synchronizing with my pulse
Rising with the Ibis's rhythmic dance
in the wind on its way up high
to the place where no cold winds blow
where thoughts cease to have meaning
and separation doesn't exist
Beyond the earth
Beyond the learnt and the known
where the undefinable, indescribable resides
in a residence without walls or beginnings or
endings
in a space that holds the world
and me and my new friend in it

References

Boye, Karin. "Yes of Course it Hurts," *For Tradet's Skull*. 1935.

Chödrön, Pema. *Taking a Leap*. 2004.

———. *When Things Fall Apart*. 1997.

———. *The Wisdom of No Escape*. 2001.

Dahlgren, Eva. "Jag År Gud." 1991.

Draper, Dar. *What is Love? Questions a Child Asks*, illustrated by Sarah Dawn Helser, 2004.

Einstein, Albert. Essay in *Living Philosophies*. New York: Simon & Schuster, 1931.

————. "This I Believe," essay for a radio broadcast series. 1950.

Ekdahl, Lisa. "Jag Tar Vara på Vattnet Då Åskan Går." 2004.

European Organization for Nuclear Research, https:// home.cern/science/physics/dark-matter.

"Forests," *Our Planet*. Directed by Jeff Wilson, narrated by David Attenborough.

Gibran, Kahlil. *The Prophet: On Death*. 1923.

Hjalmarsson, Helena. *Finding Lina*. 2013.

————. *Beyond Autism*. 2019.

Keats, John, excerpt from a letter to his brothers, dated December 22, 1817.

Komunyakaa, Yusef, "Anodyne," reprinted from Poetry Society of America's Award Ceremony Program. 2007.

Live Science, September 22, 2020.

Lobel, Arnold. *Frog and Toad Together*. 1972.

Millay, Edna St. Vincent. *Renascence and other Poems*. 1917.

Moskowitz, Clara. "Dark Matter May Feel a 'Dark Force' That the Rest of the Universe Does Not." *Scientific American*, April 20, 2015.

Muller, F. Max. *Dhammapada, The Sayings of Buddha*. 2021.

Neruda, Pablo. "It is Born," *Fully Empowered*. 2001.

———. *The Sea and the Bells*. 1988.

———. *Extravagaria*. 2001.

Oliver, Mary. "The Journey," *Dream Work*. 1986.

Ruiz, Don Miguel. *Mastery of Love*. 1999.

Rumi. "The Thirsty Fish," "Quietness," "Wax," "A Community of the Spirit," "Dance in Your Blood," "Birdwings," *The Essential Rumi*, translated by Coleman Barks. 2004.

Selassie, Haile. Speech to the United Nations. 1967.

Singer, Michael A. *The Untethered Soul*. 2007.

Walker, Alice. "The Gospel According to Shug," *The Temple of My Familiar*. 1989.

AUTHOR BIO

HELENA HJALMARSSON, MA, LCSW, LP, is a psychoanalyst and NeuroMovement® practitioner in North Salem, NY. Her practices are informed by the idea of non-duality, the power of the present moment and the freedom that can be found by reaching beyond one's personal identity, experience and beliefs. Helena is the author of *Finding Lina* (Skyhorse 2013) and *Beyond Autism* (Skyhorse 2019). She lives in North Salem, NY, with her two daughters.